FROM THE
SHADOWS
—— INTO THE ——
LIGHT

BREAKING FREE
FROM STIGMA AND SCANDAL

—— BestSelling Author ——
CONNIE PAGLIANITI

I dedicate this book to my beautiful mum, whose love, strength, and unwavering belief in me never wavered. I carry you with me always.

"This book would not have been possible without the love, support, and strength of the people who stood by me through my darkest moments and believed in me when I struggled to believe in myself.

To my husband, **David**, thank you for your patience, your love, and for standing by my side when life was at its toughest. Your quiet strength carried me in ways you may never fully realize.

To my son, **Tristan**, you are my reason for everything. Your love and resilience gave me the strength to fight, to heal, and to rebuild. I hope this book serves as a reminder that no matter what life throws at us, we always have the power to rise.

To my beautiful **mum**, now in heaven, I miss you every single day. Your love, sacrifices, and unwavering belief in me gave me the strength to keep going. I know you're watching over me, and I hope I'm making you proud.

To my **friends**, too many to mention, the ones who never left my side, even when I had lost my way—your belief in me gave me the courage to keep going. Thank you for standing in the storm with me.

To my **lawyer, David**, thank you for fighting for me when I couldn't fight for myself. Your guidance and support made a difference in ways words can't fully express.

To **Gambler's Help and ReSPIN Program**, thank you for allowing me to share my story and use my experiences to help others. Your work is changing lives, and I am grateful to be part of a community that provides hope and support to those in need.

To **Kaley Chu**, my mentor and guide in the world of public speaking—thank you for pushing me beyond my comfort zone, believing in me, and helping me find my voice on stage. Your wisdom and encouragement have been invaluable.

To **She Rises Studios, Hanna Olivas, and her amazing team**, thank you for giving me this opportunity to share my story. Your platform is changing lives, and I am honored to be part of this incredible movement.

And to **anyone who has ever felt lost, ashamed, or beyond redemption**—this book is for you. You are not alone, and your story is far from over."

Table of Contents

Introduction

My journey hasn't been perfect—far from it. It's been messy, painful, and at times, unbearably hard. But if there's one thing I've learned, it's that even in our darkest moments, there is always a way forward. *From the Shadows into the Light* is my story of falling, breaking, and finding the courage to rebuild—not just my life, but my sense of self.

For years, I lived behind a carefully crafted image of success, hiding a painful secret—my struggle with gambling addiction. I thought I had it all under control, until one day, I didn't. When my world collapsed, I lost more than my career and reputation. I lost my freedom. I lost myself. But prison wasn't the end of my story—it was the beginning of something I never expected: clarity, healing, and an unshakable determination to turn my pain into purpose.

Too often, society defines people by their worst moments. But we are not our mistakes. We are not the labels others give us. We are who we choose to become after the fall. This book isn't just about my journey—it's about all of us who have ever felt ashamed, judged, or stuck in the past. If you've ever wondered if it's possible to start over, I promise you—it is.

If you're ready to step out of the shadows and into a life filled with hope and possibility, then this book is for you. Let's walk this path together

Chapter 1

The Reckoning: From Calabria to Redemption

The knock echoed through the house, sharp and deliberate, as though it already knew it was about to dismantle my world. My son opened the door, and there he was—a stranger holding an envelope I had feared for so long. 'Connie Paglianiti,' he said flatly, 'you've been served.'

I froze momentarily, the weight of those words crushing the air around me. Without thinking, I snatched the envelope from his hands and bolted to my room. My heart pounded, my hands trembling as I slammed the door behind me. My husband and son followed, their voices cutting through the fog of panic.

'What is it, Connie? What have you been served with?' my husband demanded, his tone sharp but tinged with confusion and fear. I sat on the edge of the bed, the envelope clenched in my hands like a bomb about to explode. Finally, I tore it open, and with it, the illusion I had so desperately fought to maintain fell away. It wasn't just the beginning of my unravelling—it was the moment I knew I couldn't run anymore. This was my reckoning.

Shame clawed at my throat as I finally whispered the words I had been too terrified to admit. This was the end—or so I thought. It was the beginning of a journey I could never have imagined—a journey through guilt, resilience, and ultimately, redemption.

As I sat clutching the envelope, my mind drifted to the foundations of my life—where it all began. Calabria, a small town tucked away in southern Italy, was where my story started, long before the choices that led me to this moment. In those simpler times, life was shaped by resilience, discipline, and the unrelenting push to survive. It was in that place, amidst hardship and hope, that the seeds of the woman I would become were planted.***

In the heart of Italy's rugged landscapes, nestled within the embrace of Calabria, lies a small town that time seems to have forgotten. Born into this dwindling community in the late 1950s, my story begins amidst its narrow streets and fading memories. Once home to 1,500 souls, our town now barely whispers the tales of the 600 who remain, a stark testament to the relentless march of time. The shops that once dotted our streets, a dozen in their prime, have all vanished, leaving behind echoes of laughter and commerce that my childhood never knew.

We resided in a modest, compact house composed of just one room. My parents occupied one double bed, while I shared another with my brother and two sisters. Adjacent to this room was a tiny kitchenette, equipped with an open fire for cooking and a cooktop that featured two burners fuelled by gas cylinders. The house lacked plumbing, necessitating the use of a chamber pot for our sanitary needs, which we cleaned out each day. Additionally, there was no running water on the property; thus, my mother had to make regular trips to the town centre to fetch water. Our home was perched on a cliff— not far from a water source, yet fetching water was a strenuous task for my petite mother, who struggled with the weight of the heavy buckets on her climb back home.

Although I do not personally recall the incident, the story of how I acquired the burn mark on my elbow has been recounted to me numerous times. It happened on my second birthday, a chilly winter day. My mother had kindled the fire before leaving briefly to collect water from the fountain. During her absence, I somehow ended up amidst the flames. By the time she returned, my clothes and hair had been singed, leaving me with a burn on my elbow as the sole significant injury. I was immediately rushed to the doctor, who treated the burn with a special cream. Despite the years that have passed, the scar on my right elbow remains a vivid reminder of that day.

It was not until the mid-1960s that our living situation saw some improvement when my parents took over another room downstairs. They constructed an internal staircase to connect the two levels, which afforded us slightly more space. Despite this expansion, I still shared my bed with my siblings, and we now had a dining table where we could gather for family meals.

Around the same period, our humble home finally received some modern upgrades. Plumbing was installed in the kitchenette, which dramatically changed our daily routines. In this small kitchen space, we also installed a toilet, presenting a new challenge: Whenever someone needed to use the toilet, everyone else had to leave the kitchen. This setup, although an improvement, certainly made for some unique family dynamics and required a bit of coordination during our daily activities.

My earliest memories are not of play or youthful mischief but of a harsh reality that moulded me from a tender age. My father, a figure of unyielding expectations, believed in discipline over affection. The slightest misstep, as innocuous as a shattered glass, would unleash a storm of rebukes and beatings. These were my formative lessons, taught not with words of encouragement but with the sting of a hand or belt. Play was a luxury afforded to others, not to me. My afternoons were not spent in the embrace of childish adventures but in the toil of our farm, assisting my mother in tasks far beyond my years.

We were a family bound not by wealth but by necessity and resilience. The clothes on our backs were the product of our own hands, each stitch a testament to our resourcefulness. By the age of six, I had learned to cook, a skill born not of passion but of necessity. Life was a cycle of mundane tasks, punctuated only by the fleeting joy of companionship with my best friend who lived next door.

My father's absences, though a cause for loneliness in our home, were a bittersweet respite. His journeys to the north or across the borders of Switzerland and France meant peace from his harsh discipline. The return of my father was eagerly anticipated for one reason alone—the chocolates he brought back. In those moments, the sweetness of chocolate was a rare escape from the bitterness of my reality.

Our celebrations diverged from the norm. Christmas, as the world celebrated on December 25th, was not our day of festivity. Instead, we awaited January 6th, the day of Epiphany, when La Befana, the good witch of folklore, would visit. It was a night of simple joys, with homemade sweets or nocciolini (hazelnuts) left in a sock by our beds, a magical respite from our daily struggles. On Epiphany day, we played with the nocciolini with our friends, and the winner took all of them. Almost always, I won them.

My days began with the dawn, as I went to school and returned to the farm by afternoon. There, alongside my mother, I would collect olives to press into oil and bake bread that would sustain us for weeks. The aroma of fresh bread and the taste of our olive oil were small comforts in a life that was anything but easy.

Despite the hardships, there were moments of fleeting dreams and aspirations. The arrival of our first television set in 1967, a modest black-and-white portal to a world beyond our own, ignited in me a passion for the arts. The figures dancing and singing on the screen spoke to a part of me that yearned for expression and escape. I dreamed of singing and acting, of stepping beyond the confines of my reality into a realm where my voice could be heard. Yet, in the shadows of our small, dwindling town, such dreams seemed as distant as the stars.

As I navigated the complexities of my childhood, I learned the harsh lessons of resilience and hope. Life in Calabria was not about the dreams one dared to dream but about the realities one had to face. Yet, within me burned a desire for more, a determination to break the chains of my circumstances and forge a path of my own. This is my journey, a tale of breaking chains and seeking light in the darkness of a small town in Calabria.

In the waning months of 1967, a pivotal decision was made by my father that would irrevocably alter the trajectory of our family's life. Motivated by a vision of a more prosperous future for his four children, he resolved to leave our quaint village in Italy for the expansive opportunities of Australia. Fortuitously, a family friend who had previously emigrated and settled there offered to sponsor our move, paving the way for a new beginning in a land far from our own.

The journey commenced in earnest in September 1968 when my father boarded the illustrious *Flotta Lauro*. This ship, renowned for its opulent interiors and cutting-edge facilities, set the gold standard in migrant transport and symbolised the modern life that awaited us across the seas. Determined to establish a stable foundation for us, he wanted to personally ensure that Australia could offer the promising future he envisioned.

Upon his arrival, he was immediately taken by the vibrant landscapes and welcoming culture of Australia. He wasted no time in securing employment, saving every penny with diligent precision to cover his initial expenses, and preparing a home where his family could thrive. By the end of January 1969, everything was set for the rest of us to join him.

The announcement of our impending move struck me with a profound sense of loss. At eleven years old, leaving behind everything familiar—my cousins, friends, and the only life I knew—was excruciating. The fabric of my world was unravelling, each thread pulling away toward an unknown destination. My heartache was only briefly alleviated during our journey to Sicily, where we were to board the majestic *Galileo Galilei* for our voyage to Australia.

As I stood at the edge of the Sicilian dock, I encountered the ocean for the first time. It was not just a body of water but a vast expanse that stretched to the horizon, merging seamlessly with the sky. The colours were unlike anything I had seen before—shades of deep blue interspersed with sparkling aquamarine that danced under the sun's watchful eye. The surface of the sea shimmered with a million diamonds as the sunlight kissed the waves.

The sea's vastness was overwhelming, almost intimidating, yet it beckoned with a mysterious allure. The rhythmic sound of the waves crashing against the shore played a soothing melody, while the salty breeze brushed against my face, leaving whispers of maritime secrets in its wake. Standing there, I felt as if I were on the brink of a great adventure, peering into the abyss of the unknown. The sea seemed to promise infinite possibilities, its depths holding stories of explorers and adventurers who had charted its waters in search of new lands and treasures.

In that moment, my sorrow was tempered by a budding curiosity and a flicker of excitement. The immense sea laid before me a path to a new beginning, a canvas vast and empty, ready to be painted with the experiences and dreams of what lay ahead. It was a bittersweet farewell to my past, anchored in the hope of discovering what wonders awaited beyond the horizon.

As *Galileo Galilei* sounded its horn, a deep, resonant call that seemed to echo across the water, I turned my gaze forward. The ship, a colossal figure against the backdrop of the expansive sea, was ready to carry us into a future as wide and as deep as the ocean itself. The sight of it, powerful and reassuring, solidified my resolve. With each wave we would soon traverse, I was stepping further into a new chapter of my life, one that was both daunting and thrilling in its sheer immensity.

The 28-day crossing aboard *Galileo Galilei* was nothing short of a revelation, transforming what could have been a monotonous journey into a voyage of endless fascination. The ship was not merely a mode of transport; it was a floating city brimming with wonders, a microcosm of the world I had only dreamt of exploring.

Each morning, as the sun cast its golden hues over the endless sea, the vessel came alive with the vibrant buzz of activity. The cinemas, with their plush velvet seats and grand silver screens, were portals to other worlds. They offered daily escapes into stories of far-off lands and thrilling adventures, captivating my imagination and leaving me wide-eyed with excitement.

The theatres were equally mesmerising, their stages lit with dazzling lights and adorned with elaborate sets that changed nightly. Here, actors in exquisite costumes played out dramas and comedies, their voices echoing through the halls, stirring emotions and drawing applause from an audience as diverse as the ocean's own treasures.

At night, the nightclubs on the upper decks pulsated with the rhythms of music from around the globe. The air was thick with the sounds of laughter and the clinking of glasses, as people danced under the stars. The atmosphere was charged with an electrifying energy that made it impossible not to feel a part of something grand and exhilarating.

The restaurants aboard were a feast for the senses, each offering a different culinary adventure. From the aromatic spices of the East to the robust flavours of the Mediterranean, each meal was a celebration of the regions we sailed past. The lavish swimming pools offered a cool respite during the day, their waters mirroring the azure of the sky and sea, a surreal experience of swimming atop the deep blue, floating between the heavens and the deep.

Each day aboard *Galileo Galilei* brought discoveries that captivated my youthful imagination and expanded my understanding of the world. The ship was a labyrinth of luxury and excitement, each corner and corridor holding a new secret to be uncovered, each sunset viewed from its decks a reminder of the vastness of the world and the limitless possibilities it held.

This journey was more than a crossing; it was an initiation into the mysteries and marvels of life beyond my small Italian village. As the ship carved its path across the cerulean depths, I stood at the rail, spellbound by the endless horizon, forever changed by the wonders I had witnessed.

During the voyage aboard *Galileo Galilei*, a serendipitous encounter presented itself that would linger in my memory for years to come. One evening, while wandering through the ship's elegantly appointed dining hall, I spotted a waiter whose striking resemblance to Little Tony, my favourite Italian singer, was uncanny. Little Tony, known for his dark, wavy hair that framed his face perfectly, piercing blue eyes that seemed to hold a world of stories, and a velvety voice that could melt hearts, was an icon of Italian music. His songs had been the soundtrack to many of my childhood days, filling them with melody and dreams.

The waiter, with his similar jet-black hair and those distinct, deep blue eyes, moved through the dining hall with a grace that seemed too refined for his role. When he greeted me, his voice had the soft, melodious undertone that was eerily reminiscent of Little Tony's singing voice. It was almost as if the singer had stepped out of the television screen and into reality, choosing to masquerade as a simple waiter aboard a ship crossing the vast ocean.

Despite his repeated assurances that he was just another crew member, a part of me couldn't shake off the delightful conspiracy that had formed in my mind. I imagined that perhaps Little Tony, weary of the relentless demands of fame and the unending public adoration, had sought a temporary escape under an assumed identity. Maybe he craved the anonymity that came with such a role, yearning for a respite where his persona could be as unremarkable as the endless waves we sailed upon.

Throughout the voyage, I would often seek him out under the pretence of needing assistance, just to hear him speak or watch the way he interacted with other passengers. Each encounter added layers to my silent narrative, constructing a delightful fantasy where the celebrated singer shared snippets of an ordinary life, far removed from the glare of the spotlight.

This intriguing interlude added a touch of magic to my journey, weaving a thread of mystery and enchantment through the days at sea. Whether he was indeed Little Tony or merely a doppelgänger blessed with similar features, he became a symbol of the unexpected joys and playful escapades that travel could bring, enriching my experience with the allure of possibility and the charm of a secret only I seemed to know.

My adventures aboard *Galileo Galilei* were not merely confined to those innocent musings about the celebrity-like waiter. During the voyage, I befriended a family with a vivacious teenage daughter who was accompanied by her doting boyfriend. Though my mother often ushered us into the children's playroom, my spirit craved adventure over confinement. Each time she relaxed her vigilant watch, I seized the opportunity to explore the ship's many wonders.

I would sneak out to immerse myself in the latest movies being shown in the ship's cinema, where stories from different corners of the world came alive on the big screen, or I would simply lounge by the side of one of the ship's grand swimming pools. There, surrounded by joyful chatter and the refreshing splashes of water, I absorbed the lively atmosphere of the ship, each moment adding to my growing sense of independence and curiosity.

However, one fateful day, my thirst for adventure led to an unfortunate misunderstanding that would linger in my memory. While by the poolside, I attempted to mimic the adults around me, playfully massaging the shoulders of the teenage girl's boyfriend. My actions, innocent though they were, aimed only to emulate the relaxed interactions I observed. This scene, however, was misinterpreted by my mother, who, in a flush of concern and misunderstanding, delivered a swift and stern reprimand. Her hand struck my face with a sharp slap that resonated with a startling loudness, drawing the eyes of all around us.

The incident left me deeply mortified. The public chastisement stung sharply, and I spent the remainder of the day hidden away in a secluded nook of the ship, nursing my embarrassment and the sting of public disapproval. In that quiet solitude, I reflected on the complexities of growing up, the fine line between innocent exploration and the perception of impropriety.

This voyage, marked by both wonder and moments of youthful indiscretion, was not merely a journey across the ocean but the beginning of a much larger journey within. It was a transformative passage that would challenge and change us in countless ways as we transitioned from our old lives in a small Italian village to a new world brimming with possibilities in Australia. Each wave that the ship cleaved on its path seemed to carry away the remnants of our past, ushering in waves of new experiences and lessons that would shape our futures.

Our maritime journey brought us around Africa and finally to the shores of Australia, where our first port of call was in Fremantle. The city of Fremantle, with its bustling streets and the novelty of modern conveniences, offered us our first taste of Australian life. One of the most mesmerising experiences was encountering escalators for the first time. The sight of these moving stairs, so commonplace yet so alien to us, left us both amused and enchanted. We spent hours riding them up and down, marvelling at this simple yet magical form of transportation that epitomised the modernity we were stepping into.

However, our visit to Fremantle was nearly marred by a moment of panic when preparing to return to the ship, my mother realised she had forgotten our passports onboard. Fortunately, our distress was short-lived, thanks to a friendly waiter from the ship who had served us throughout the voyage. Recognising us immediately, he quickly offered his assistance. With a reassuring smile, he dashed back to our cabin and retrieved the passports, bringing them down to my anxious mother at the pier. His kindness and swift action spared us a great deal of trouble and solidified my first impressions of the generous spirit of the people in this new land.

Our journey continued with a brief stop in Adelaide. My memories of Adelaide are overshadowed by the peculiar scent that seemed to permeate the air, an unexpected welcome that led me to decide against exploring the city. I remember little else but the relief of returning to the ship, eager to leave the lingering odours behind.

Finally, we arrived in Melbourne, where our first glimpse from the water was of the beautifully lit skyline. The city lights twinkled like stars against the night sky, a stunning display that heralded the beginning of our new life. As we approached Station Pier, the cool sea breeze carried the sounds and scents of this bustling metropolis, weaving them into the fabric of my first memories of what would soon become my home. Standing on the deck, watching Melbourne come closer with each passing moment, I felt a surge of hope and excitement for the future that awaited us here.

Chapter 2

Echoes of Dreams: Navigating New Worlds

From the deck of the ship, as it docked in Melbourne, I spotted my father and a group of people energetically waving at us. Their familiar faces sparked a surge of excitement and relief after the long voyage. Once we navigated through the procedures of customs and immigration, Dad enveloped us in a warm comforting embrace—a feeling of homecoming that extended to the kisses and hugs from the friends who had gathered. These were friends from our hometown who had ventured to Australia years earlier, their presence making our arrival less daunting and more like a reunion.

We piled into their cars, which whisked us away to our new home in Preston. The journey there was filled with wide-eyed wonder as I marvelled at the sprawling houses with their lush gardens, a stark contrast to the cramped conditions we had left behind. As we pulled up to the house that Dad had rented for us, my excitement grew—the house was unlike anything I had ever seen.

Stepping inside, I was taken aback by the sheer space: three bedrooms, a bathroom, a lounge, a dining room, a kitchen, and even a sunroom. The backyard was enormous, complete with a separate laundry and an outdoor toilet. It felt as if all our Christmases had come at once. Though I still had to share a bedroom with two of my siblings—my brother being the only boy who received his own room—I finally had my own single bed.

The house was modestly furnished, yet everything seemed luxurious to me. There was a fridge, which was a novelty I had never encountered before, that kept food cool. The lounge suite, dining table, and chairs might have been simple, but to me, they were regal. But what excited me most was the amazingly large black and white TV set in the living room. It was like a portal to another world, bringing images and sounds from across the globe right into our new home. Living in a fully furnished house with appliances and furniture that seemed fit for royalty, and this magical machine that flickered with life, was a dramatic and delightful shift from our previous existence.

Each room held the promise of new beginnings, and the space felt like a canvas on which we could paint our new lives in Australia.

Mum and Dad were illiterate, so their employment opportunities were severely limited. Dad took on two jobs, not only to cover all of our trips, including his own, but also to manage the rent and furniture payments and keep four children fed. I suspect the excitement of reuniting with Mum after such a long separation overwhelmed Dad because exactly nine months after our arrival, another sibling—the only 'skip' in the family—was born.

Dad worked tirelessly, often seven days a week for long hours, to make ends meet. While his absence was a hardship, it carried a silver lining for me. With Dad not around to impose strict rules, I had the freedom to indulge in one of the small luxuries of our new life: watching TV. I still vividly remember that Saturday morning, just a few days after our arrival, when I was glued to the television, watching a music show on Channel 0, which I would later come to know as *Update '69*.

That particular morning, a young man in a suit, holding an umbrella while rain seemingly poured over him, appeared on the screen. Not understanding English at the time, I assumed the song was about the rain. But the language barrier did nothing to prevent my instant infatuation with him. Although it was a black-and-white TV set, the brightness of his features made it clear he had blonde hair and blue eyes. I was utterly smitten. From that day on, he became my knight in shining armour. His voice seemed magical, his looks surpassed those of Adonis, and he exuded the aura of a genuinely kind-hearted young man.

He was the whole package, at least in the eyes of a young girl who had just landed on the shores of a new country. He epitomised what I believed every Australian male would look like—an assumption that, unfortunately, I would soon realise was far from reality. As I began to explore more of Melbourne and meet a broader spectrum of its residents, it became evident that the diversity here was far greater than what my youthful fantasies had portrayed. This realisation was a part of growing up and adjusting my expectations to align with the rich tapestry of cultures and appearances that truly defined my new home.

From that day forward, all I could think about was Johnny Farnham. He had captured my imagination on the television screen, and suddenly he was everywhere in my thoughts. His music became a backdrop to my new life in Melbourne, offering a sense of familiarity and comfort as I navigated the complexities of adjusting to a new culture and language.

My educational journey in Melbourne began at Preston East Primary School, where a family friend was also enrolled. To ensure I had a familiar face nearby, my parents placed me in grade four alongside her, despite my being of age for grade six. Unknown to my parents, I soon sought the company of other children from various nationalities. My goal was to immerse myself in English rather than sticking to Italian, which I could speak at home.

One figure who remains vivid in my memory is Mr. Gow, my grade four teacher. His kindness and patience were instrumental during my transition. He dedicated extra time to help me grasp the nuances of English, a language that felt so foreign at first. His efforts were not in vain; I quickly excelled in mathematics, where numbers provided a universal language that I mastered with ease. Spelling presented more of a challenge due to my initial unfamiliarity with English, but within six months, I had surged to the top of my class in this area as well.

Despite being placed in specialised English classes meant to aid my linguistic transition, I found them frustratingly basic. I was eager to dive into more complex vocabulary, not revisit the rudimentary words suitable for a grade one level. The curriculum, in general, seemed far less challenging than what I was accustomed to in Italy. The material we covered in grade four in Australia had already been taught in grade two back home, and by the time we reached grade six, I recognised it as the content of Italy's grade three curriculum. This disparity only fueled my determination to seek out more stimulating educational experiences and solidify my command of the English language.

One weekend, when the family of my school friend came to visit us, my parents were curious about how I was adjusting to school. They asked her how I was doing, to which she unexpectedly responded that she didn't know because I wouldn't speak to her. My parents were taken aback by this and pressed me for an explanation. I candidly told them that she always spoke to me in Italian at school, and I was determined to learn English instead.

Thankfully, they understood my reasoning and, in a welcome change from the past, I was not reprimanded or punished for my decision.

I cherished my time at school; it was not just a place for learning but also a sanctuary where I could forge friendships and immerse myself in the English language, which once seemed so alien to me. Among my peers, I developed a particularly close bond with a Greek girl named Mary. She was a wonderful friend, and we became inseparable during school hours, sharing everything from lunchtime treats to secrets.

However, my contentment was abruptly disrupted six months before we were set to finish primary school. My parents, seizing an opportunity to improve our living situation, purchased a small house in Thornbury. While this move was a positive step for our family, it meant leaving behind the school I had grown to love and the friends I had made. The prospect of moving schools so close to the end of primary school was daunting. I was saddened by the thought of having to start anew, with very little time left to adapt or form new friendships before transitioning to secondary education.

This unexpected change weighed heavily on me as I faced the challenge of entering a new school environment, where I would have to quickly establish myself and connect with new classmates under the pressure of impending graduation. It was a testing time, pushing me to find resilience and adaptability I hadn't known I possessed.

It was hard to grasp how, in just a few short years, I had lost connections with my dear friends, all due to drastic changes that occurred without my input or consent. Each move and transition felt like an upheaval, uprooting me just as I began to settle in and form meaningful relationships. This pattern of sudden changes left me feeling a profound sense of loss, as each relocation seemed to strip away the friendships that had become my anchor in a constantly shifting world.

Adjusting to my new school in Thornbury proved challenging, as many students had formed tight-knit groups since the beginning of their schooling. For a newcomer like me, it was daunting to try and infiltrate these established circles. The sense of being an outsider was palpable, making those initial days both lonely and difficult.

Despite these hurdles, I found a silver lining. A handful of students were slated to attend the same high school as I was. This common future allowed us to connect on a more immediate basis, and we began to forge what started as tentative friendships. These relationships, initially formed out of necessity and shared circumstance, gradually deepened as we moved together into high school.

Remarkably, a few of these friendships, born out of those challenging early days at my new school, have endured over the years. They have grown alongside me, becoming a cherished part of my life and a reminder of how initial adversity can lead to lasting bonds.

In 1973, Johnny Farnham was starring in the stage show *Pippin*, and I knew I simply couldn't miss it. Given that my parents were incredibly strict, only allowing me to leave the house for school, I had to get creative if I wanted to catch the show. Seizing the opportunity, I decided to skip school on a Wednesday afternoon, the only time I could possibly sneak away to see the play.

The performance was everything I had hoped for and more, but it posed a logistical challenge: It finished well after school hours, leaving me with the tricky task of returning home after both of my parents had already arrived from work. In a bid for stealth, I resorted to sneaking in through the bedroom window. To cover for my tardy return, my siblings, complicit in my escapade, would tell our parents that I was busy doing my homework, should they ask.

This little adventure, risky as it was, gave me a thrilling taste of independence and a memorable afternoon immersed in the magic of live theatre, watching my idol perform on stage. I was so captivated by *Pippin* and Johnny Farnham's performance that I found myself returning to see the show on three separate occasions. Each trip was a thrilling escape, filled with anticipation and excitement as I immersed myself once again in the vibrant atmosphere of the theatre.

On my second visit, a stroke of luck brought me an unexpected new friend and a cherished memory. While waiting by the stage door, hoping for a glimpse of my idol, I struck up a conversation with a lovely young lady named Anne from Adelaide. She noticed the autograph book clutched in my hands and kindly offered to help. With a smile, she took the book inside and returned with Johnny Farnham's signature gracing its pages—a treasure I would hold dear forever.

The pinnacle of my theatrical escapades came on my third visit. That afternoon, I not only saw the show but also had the incredible fortune of meeting Johnny Farnham himself. Standing there, face to face with the man whose voice had enchanted me from the first note, I was overcome with shyness. Words escaped me, and all I could muster was a timid 'Hi.' Despite my overwhelming nerves, that moment of brief interaction was a dream come true.

The issue of physical violence from my father didn't cease after moving to this country. I recall a particularly harrowing evening when my mother was hospitalised, and I was left in charge of cooking for my four siblings. However, longing for a moment of childhood play, I made a decision that would have painful consequences. Instead of cooking, I peeled some potatoes and hid them at the bottom of the rubbish bin, placing the peels on top to give the appearance that I had cooked them. That night, we had sandwiches for dinner.

Unfortunately, when my father returned home, one of my siblings told him the truth about the dinner. He checked the bin, saw the peels, and was then informed that the whole potatoes were underneath. What followed was a frightening display of anger. My father, unhindered by the absence of my mother, used whatever he could lay his hands on—be it the buckle of his belt, an extension cord, or his own fists and feet—to discipline me.

I was left black and blue after these incidents—bruises that I hid from the world. I never shared what was happening at home with any of my friends. From an early age, I learned to erect an emotional shield, concealing my pain and the shame that accompanied it. This silence became a heavy burden, one that I carried discreetly throughout my childhood.

In primary school, I always chose to wear long pants and long-sleeved tops, a wardrobe carefully selected to cover the marks that I couldn't let anyone see. High school brought its own challenges with uniforms that varied with the seasons. The summer and winter themes meant shorter sleeves during warmer months, which made it harder to keep my bruises hidden.

From an early age, sewing was not just a skill for me but a necessary craft that I honed under the guidance of a local dressmaker after moving to Australia. My mother, having grown up without a mother herself, lacked the experience to guide me through the transitions from girlhood to womanhood. Recognising her own limitations, she introduced me to a dressmaker who became more than just a mentor in sewing; she also became the person who explained the changes my body would undergo as I matured.

This dressmaker, though initially a stranger, took on the delicate task of explaining the menstrual cycle to me—a topic that was never discussed openly in our family. We never talked about the birds and the bees at home, and everything I knew about such matters came piecemeal from overheard conversations among friends.

Continuing to sew and create clothing for my siblings, I found comfort in the precise and familiar motions of stitching and cutting, a contrast to the complexity and mystery of the conversations about adolescence. Sewing became a grounding force in my life, a steady constant amid the whirlwind of growing up.

Sewing, a practical skill learned in childhood, transformed into a source of income during my early teens. One of our neighbours, impressed by my proficiency, hired me to teach their daughter how to sew. They paid me $15 for each lesson, which lasted a couple of hours. I carefully saved this money, keeping it hidden from my parents. Instead of spending it frivolously, I used it to fund private singing lessons from a teacher in Northcote, investing in another passion of mine.

I would head straight to the singing lessons after school, spending an hour immersed in music before rushing home to beat my parents' return. The singing teacher was a kind woman with a peculiar living situation that made the lessons memorable for reasons beyond music. She was an avid cat lover, and her home was overrun with cats. Unfortunately, this led to a less-than-pleasant environment as the scent of cat urine permeated the carpets.

Practising breathing exercises in her aromatic living room was a challenge; the overwhelming smell nearly made me nauseous on several occasions. Despite the odorous setting, the joy and fulfilment I derived from singing and improving my vocal skills made each visit worthwhile. The experience taught me not only about music but also about persevering through less-than-ideal circumstances to pursue my interests.

Part of my journey in taking singing lessons was the unique opportunity to perform in revues at various RSL clubs, mental institutions, and other venues where we entertained diverse audiences. These performances were scheduled for weekends, presenting a significant challenge as it required me to find ways to leave the house without arousing my parents' suspicions. Eventually, I realised that sneaking out was not sustainable, and I decided to be upfront with them about my activities.

Unfortunately, my honesty was met with disapproval. My parents held very traditional views and were particularly concerned about the reputation and perceived implications of a young woman entering the entertainment industry, which they deemed suitable only for 'women of the world.' They were adamant that such a path was not fitting for their daughter, influenced heavily by their old-fashioned ideas about propriety and the potential for gossip in our community.

Reluctantly, I had to respect their wishes, which meant missing out on several performances that could have furthered my experience and growth in singing. This restriction left me feeling stifled and frustrated, as my aspirations were curtailed by the weight of cultural expectations and the fear of what others might think. It was a stark reminder of the delicate balance between pursuing personal dreams and navigating the conservative values of my family background.

As I navigated the delicate balance between my family's expectations and my own aspirations, I seized every opportunity to entertain, carefully navigating around my parents' restrictions without their knowledge. Each secret performance was not just a thrilling escape but also a cherished act of defiance and self-expression. These moments not only honed my skills as a performer but also strengthened my resolve to pursue my dreams, despite the obstacles. The challenges I faced during this period taught me invaluable lessons about perseverance, the art of secrecy, and the complexities of familial love. Though constrained, these experiences were crucial in shaping the person I was becoming, preparing me for the broader horizons that lay ahead.

As this chapter of my life closes, with its mix of joyous performances and painful restrictions, a new chapter beckons. It promises new freedoms, new challenges, and the continuation of my journey in music and self-discovery. As I step into this new phase, I carry with me the lessons learned from the past—each note sung in secrecy echoing into the future, each whispered lyric a reminder of the journey thus far and the path yet to travel.

Chapter 3

Turning Points

April 11, 1973, marked a poignant shift in my journey, a day woven with threads of joy and despair that would forever alter the course of my life. It was a Wednesday afternoon when the news broadcast that Johnny Farnham, the man whose music had enchanted me, married his sweetheart. This event, though a celebration of love, felt like a personal loss, shattering the youthful fantasies that had long comforted me.

As I watched the joyful announcements unfold on every channel, the realisation that my dreams were just ephemeral fantasies struck me with unbearable clarity. In a moment of profound despair, believing that all that I had hoped for was irretrievably lost, I made a desperate choice. I took a stack of pills, seeking escape from a future I could not imagine living without the dreams that had sustained me. Miraculously, the attempt was not serious, and I emerged only slightly ill but with a new perspective on life.

This incident, though harrowing, was a critical turning point. It forced me to confront the fragility of my attachments and the need to find deeper, more sustainable sources of self-worth and happiness. As I recovered from this episode, the realisation dawned on me that my life was worth living for reasons beyond the fantasies of youth. It was a moment of painful growth, pushing me to reevaluate my path and redirect my energies towards pursuits that offered real fulfilment and joy.

Despite the dramatic events of that day, my love for Johnny never waned. As the years passed, my youthful infatuation matured into a lasting admiration that has endured into my 60s. His music remains a cherished part of my life, echoing through the years as a constant reminder of my past dreams and the resilience they instilled in me.

In the wake of this awakening, I began to explore new horizons, gradually finding beauty in the every day and strength in the genuine connections I formed with others. This chapter delves into the aftermath of that fateful day, tracing my steps from the shadows of despair to the light of new beginnings as I learned to weave a tapestry of life filled with resilience and hope.

On that day, as I watched the dreams of my youth dissolve, I made a solemn vow to myself—I would never marry nor have children. The notion of marriage, as I had witnessed and experienced through the strictures imposed by my father, seemed only to entail obedience and childbearing. Having already assumed the role of a caretaker for my siblings from a tender age, I felt as though I had prematurely shouldered burdens meant for adulthood, missing out on the carefree joys that childhood should afford. This vow was not born out of fleeting emotion but from a deep-seated desire to forge a path where I could make my own choices, unbound by the traditional expectations imposed on a wife and mother.

My sixteenth birthday was approaching, a milestone I had never celebrated with much fanfare. Unlike my peers, I had never experienced the delight of a birthday party or the sweetness of a cake made just for me. So, when my parents decided to invite another family with their children to celebrate my sweet sixteen, my excitement was uncontainable.

A few days before the celebration, a family friend, known for his connections at a local brewery, offered to purchase beer at a discounted price, which my parents accepted. He arrived with the cases during the day when my parents were absent, a time when I was usually home with just my siblings.

What was meant to be a simple delivery took a dark turn. Taking advantage of the situation, he sexually assaulted me. It was a harrowing betrayal by someone I knew well—the father of a classmate of my own age. His actions shattered my trust and marred the anticipation of my birthday. The assault was abruptly interrupted by the innocent cries of my siblings, preventing further harm.

Faced with the aftermath, I chose silence. I was terrified of the consequences that telling my parents might provoke, particularly my father, whose protective nature could have driven him to violent retribution. The burden of this secret was immense, casting a long shadow over what should have been a joyous occasion.

The situation reached a tipping point when my mother proposed a visit to their home. Panicked at the thought of facing him again, I initially refused without giving a reason. My mother, puzzled by my reluctance since I had always enjoyed our visits—both for the company of his son and their newborn baby girl, pressed me for an explanation.

Eventually, the weight of my secret became too much to bear. I confided in my mother about the assault, unleashing the painful truth. She was horrified and shared my disgust, but we both knew that telling my father was not an option. To avoid any violent fallout and protect our family's peace, she devised a lie. She told my father that she had fallen out with the assailant's wife, her co-worker, which would prevent any future visits.

This lie, though protective, added another layer of complexity to the burden I carried. It was a stark lesson in the painful realities of adult life where, sometimes, maintaining peace requires silence and sacrifice. The incident left an indelible mark on my young life, teaching me about the harshness of betrayal and the strength needed to carry such a secret.

My sixteenth birthday, already overshadowed by betrayal, soured further when the other family we had invited failed to show up, offering no explanation for their absence. The disappointment was palpable; I felt utterly mortified, as though the day had conspired to underscore my loneliness.

Among the few bright spots that day was a gift that briefly lifted my spirits— a portable record player. Its vibrant red colour was as vivid as my fleeting joy. Alongside it, I received Johnny Farnham's album 'Sadie,' a record that quickly became my refuge, the songs resonating with my turbulent emotions. I played it over and over, each note—a temporary escape from the harsh realities that clouded my life.

However, even this small solace was short-lived. My father, whose temperament had always leaned more towards volatility than warmth, let his jealousy over my affection for Johnny's music boil over. In a fit of rage, he shattered the album. The vinyl, so cherished, lay in pieces—like my heart in that moment. I was devastated. The music that had been my only bright spot amidst the struggles of adolescence was taken from me in an instant.

This incident was emblematic of my father's approach to parenting—rarely showing love, often resorting to violence. It wasn't just the physical outbursts; it was the destruction of the things that brought me joy, the constant undermining of my little havens of happiness. His actions that day not only broke my treasured album but also reinforced the walls I built around my emotions, walls that kept me guarded against the volatility I had come to expect at home.

Even before the turmoil of my sixteenth birthday, I had been cultivating a life outside the confines of my tumultuous home. At 14, during school holidays, I began working alongside my mother at the factory where she ironed pyjamas. Thanks to my sewing skills, I was quickly assigned the role of a machinist, a position that paid more than my mother's due to the technical proficiency it required. My earnings were determined by the number of pieces I completed, and this piece-rate system allowed me to earn significantly. The money I made was crucial; it went directly into the family budget, helping to cover our mortgage and food expenses.

Life became a relentless cycle of school and work, each day blending into the next with little respite. Yet, this routine provided a structure and a sense of purpose that was sorely lacking at home. It was during a routine shopping trip for my school uniform, soon after my fraught birthday, that I seized another opportunity to expand my horizons. On a whim, I asked the shop manager if they were looking for sales assistants. To my delight, they were interested and offered me a trial on the spot. The trial was a success, and I was hired immediately, adding Friday evenings and Saturday mornings to my schedule, along with additional hours during school holidays.

Working in the retail shop was more than just a job; it was a liberation. I relished the environment, so different from the factory's monotony and the oppressive atmosphere at home. The work was engaging, and I quickly made friends, including a young girl who would become a lifelong best friend. The senior ladies at the shop, particularly one, who would drive me to and from work, became my mentors and guardians in this new world. Their kindness and the camaraderie among the staff were my sanctuary, providing not only employment but also a social outlet and a brief escape from domestic strife.

These experiences at the factory and the retail shop were pivotal; they not only contributed to our household financially but also allowed me to build a sense of self-worth and independence. Each day at work reinforced my resolve to carve out a better future for myself, one where I could make my own decisions and perhaps, one day, find a life far from the shadows of my father's temper and the confines of my early responsibilities.

I absolutely loved working at the retail shop; it was a sanctuary that felt like a holiday from the constraints of home life. As long as I was outside the house, I was happy, a sentiment that marked the beginning of my dual existence: the cheerful, outgoing girl in the public eye, and the sad, restricted girl at home. This dichotomy became a coping mechanism, allowing me to navigate the disparate worlds I inhabited.

Working at the shop was not just an escape from the oppressive atmosphere at home; it was a place where I could express and enjoy the livelier part of my personality. It allowed me to feel normal, to momentarily shed the sadness and restrictions of my home life. The friendships and interactions there were genuine, providing a stark contrast to the controlled environment I endured under my father's roof.

While all my school friends enjoyed holidays or met up for fun outings, I was often left behind. Invitations to birthday parties had to be declined because my strict father wouldn't allow me to attend. However, an exception came around when one of my friends was turning sixteen and hosted a slumber party. My initial request to go was met with a firm no from my dad. But my friend and her parents, understanding my situation, came over to personally assure him that it was a girls-only event and that they would supervise closely. After much persuasion, he reluctantly agreed, but on the strict condition that he would drop me off at a specified time and pick me up the next morning at 9:00 a.m.

Knowing I would have to leave early and miss out on the next day's activities, I nonetheless accepted his terms—it was this or nothing. As part of the invitation, we were asked to bring a plate, a concept I misunderstood entirely. In my Italian household, we never took food to parties; we brought gifts. So, I took a literal plate. I remember my mother's confusion when I left our home; she questioned, 'Don't they have plates?' to which I innocently replied, 'Maybe they don't have enough for everyone.'

Upon arriving at the party, I proudly handed over my empty plate, only to be met with a puzzled look from my friend. 'You were meant to bring something on the plate,' she explained. My cheeks flushed with embarrassment as I realised my mistake. It was a stark reminder of the cultural differences I was still navigating, and though it was a small misunderstanding, it left a significant imprint on me, highlighting my feelings of being an outsider even in simple social situations.

The lingering shadows of my childhood were cast by the violent hands of my father. Behind the locked doors of our lounge room, he disciplined me with a ferocity that left me wishing for escape, not just from the pain, but from life itself. His methods were harsh; not only did he use his formidable strength, but also the buckle of his belt and extension cords. The bruises and scars were hidden under my clothes—I hardly ever wore dresses to school, fearing that someone might glimpse the physical evidence of my torment.

This cycle of fear and pain continued unabated until I turned 18. That year, desperate for a reprieve, I ran away from home and went and stayed with one of my best girlfriends in Boronia. I remember catching the train from Flinders Street, at night. The night was wet and cold, and the trip was quite long. I felt lonely and scared and had tears streaming down my face. Before this, I had never ventured out at night on my own. Eventually, I got to Boronia Station, where my girlfriend's parents picked me up in their car. I loved my girlfriend's parents with all my heart. They were warm and kind, and I was forever grateful to them for taking me in.

I was only there for three days before my father found out through another girlfriend where I was staying. A phone call came through and my friend put my dad on the phone, who promised me that if I returned by the following morning, he would not punish me. The promise only lasted a few weeks. I could have gone to the police, but I didn't want to take the main provider from the family by contacting the police, who could have jailed him. My relationship with Dad remained strained and devoid of affection throughout my early years.

Being restricted from socialising and confined to a life of school and work, I found little room for joy. Italian cultural norms held tightly to the idea that girls should not venture out socially, which only deepened my isolation. From the age of 14, I worked during school holidays in the same factories as my mother, and at 16, I took a job as a shop assistant at a shop in Northcote. Here, I worked on school holidays, Friday nights, and Saturday mornings. I worked there for just over three years as a sales assistant part-time and then another three years full-time as their Personal Assistant.

As the eldest of five children, my parents couldn't afford to send me to university. Therefore, at the age of 19, I left school to seek full-time employment. Fortuitously, an opportunity arose at the retail shop where I had been working; their PA had resigned, and I eagerly applied for the position. I secured the job and embraced the chance to learn and advance. My boss recognised my enthusiasm and mentored me extensively. He entrusted me with the responsibility to run the office during his absences—a rare and significant opportunity for someone my age, and a first in his tenure.

My dreams were dashed from becoming an entertainer to even attending university. Despite not being able to pursue higher education or a career in entertainment as I had dreamed, I found solace and purpose in acting and singing. I performed in Australian TV shows, theatre productions, and at charity events. One particularly impactful experience was performing at Larundel Psychiatric Hospital in Bundoora, where I saw firsthand the devastating effects of substance abuse.

At 18, I began organising fundraising events for various charities, starting with The Spastic Society of Victoria, now known as Scope. This work sparked a passion for event planning that would shape my career.

By the age of 21, tired of the constraints imposed by my father, I declared my independence, asserting my right to enjoy life and socialise as an adult. Though he initially resisted, I persisted, and his control over me gradually diminished. At 23, I left home for good, moving into a flat with assistance from friends. This marked a new beginning, one where I could live without fear of violence.

It wasn't until I was 25 that I began to reconcile with my father, understanding that his own violent upbringing had shaped his behaviour. This realisation didn't erase the past, but it allowed me to forgive him. We never openly discussed these issues, as was typical in our culture, but this unspoken understanding helped mend our relationship.

At the age of 20, an unexpected turn of events led me to participate in a beauty pageant that aimed to raise funds for The Spastic Society of Victoria.

This organisation, established in 1952 by three parents whose children had cerebral palsy, provided essential services like sheltered workshops and day centres for individuals who were often overlooked by mainstream employment due to their disabilities. At the time, people with cerebral palsy were commonly referred to as 'spastics,' a term now recognised as inappropriate and offensive.

The pageant was not just a contest of beauty; it was a significant fundraising initiative. Without my initial knowledge, a friend had entered my name as a contestant, knowing my enthusiasm for charitable causes. This thrust me into the centre of event planning and fundraising activities, which opened my eyes to the profound challenges and societal contributions of people living with cerebral palsy.

Determined to make a meaningful impact, I threw myself into the fundraising efforts with vigour. My involvement went beyond merely participating in the pageant; I organised events that drew attention and resources to the cause. The community's response was overwhelming, and thanks to the collective efforts, we raised a substantial amount of money.

Though I was deeply involved in the fundraising, my physical appearance—being neither tall enough nor fitting the conventional 'model' look—meant that I would not represent the Italian community as its pageant queen. Instead, my role evolved into something arguably more impactful—just fundraising money to go into the pool for the person who actually represented Miss Italian Community Fund.

The funds I helped raise were pooled into the Miss Italian Community Fund, supporting the broader mission of the charity, now known as 'Scope.' While a model-looking Italian girl was chosen to represent the community outwardly, I took great pride in the substantial behind-the-scenes contributions I had made.

This experience was a defining moment in my life, reinforcing my belief in the power of community and charity. It also highlighted the often superficial nature of beauty standards, teaching me valuable lessons about the true essence of beauty and the importance of advocacy and compassion.

As I stand at the threshold of new beginnings, I reflect on the myriad challenges that shaped the contours of my youth. Each ordeal, each betrayal, and each triumph contributed to the tapestry of my life, weaving patterns of resilience and determination. From the despair of personal betrayals to the small victories in the world of work, these experiences forged my character in the fires of adversity.

My sixteenth birthday, though marked by betrayal and disappointment, was also a crucible that tested and, ultimately, strengthened my spirit. The lessons learned were harsh but invaluable, teaching me that true strength lies in the ability to navigate through life's storms, not merely to survive them but to emerge with newfound wisdom and resolve.

As I close this chapter of my life in writing, I carry forward the solemn vow I made to myself—a vow to live life on my own terms, to seek happiness in authenticity and freedom, and to never let the shadows of the past dim the light of my future. This vow, made amidst the ruins of broken dreams, has guided me like a beacon through the vicissitudes of life, leading me towards horizons filled with hope and promise.

In the narrative of my life, the threads of past pains and pleasures intertwine, leading me onward, ever pushing me towards my next chapter, where new challenges await and new victories beckon.

Chapter 4

Crossroads and Continents: Adventures and Autonomy

As soon as I turned 21, I asserted my independence from my father, declaring that I would no longer just do his bidding—I was a young adult eager to explore life. My newfound freedom was symbolised by my first car, a bright yellow Holden Gemini, affectionately nicknamed 'the yellow canary' by my friends. This car wasn't just a means of transport; it was my ticket to liberty.

Not long after getting my car, the salesman who sold it to me asked me out. Enthralled by my love for movies, I suggested a night at the drive-in, which was showing a film I was eager to see. That night, as we sat in his large car watching the movie, he reached towards me. Misinterpreting his actions, I panicked and confronted him, only to find out he was merely reaching for something in the console. My embarrassment was overwhelming, and sadly, I never saw him again, leaving me uncertain about his true intentions.

My naivety sometimes bordered on the comical. On one occasion, after a comedy show at The Last Laugh, the young man I was with kissed me as he dropped me off at home. Terrified that a kiss could lead to pregnancy, I ran from the car. Although we continued to see each other, we never discussed that night; we simply remained friends.

As I became more socially active, my father imposed strict curfews, threatening that if I wasn't home by a designated time, I shouldn't bother coming home at all. Many nights, when I missed curfew, I slept in my car, wrapped in a blanket. My mother, ever caring, would come out in the middle of the night, pleading with me to come inside.

My girlfriend and I devised a plan for our nights out—we told our parents we were staying at each other's houses but would actually spend the night in my car parked at the airport. These adventurous evenings often ended with early morning coffee on Lygon Street in Carlton.

I insisted on transparency when it came to dating. Whenever I had a date, the gentlemen were introduced to, at least, my mother. One day, concerned about neighbourhood gossip, my mother confronted me. She was worried about what people would think of me going out with different men. I confidently assured her, 'Mum, I don't care what they say. I'm not doing anything wrong. I'm just enjoying dinner or dancing. They should worry more about their own daughters.'

After three years of full-time work at the retail shop, I felt a compelling need for a change. I resigned to pursue my passion for acting. I started working as a promotional girl, choosing jobs that offered flexible hours. This flexibility allowed me to start acting as an extra in various television shows produced by Crawford Productions, such as *The Sullivans*, where I was practically a regular, appearing from the first to the last episode. Although my debut on screen was just a glimpse of my nose on a tram, it was thrilling. I also participated in shows like *Cop Shop* and *Skyways*, and the producers even provided taxis for us extras—a touch of glamour and appreciation.

My acting pursuits led me to classes at the William Bates Academy, culminating in a role in one of his plays, *The Final Game*, where I portrayed a middle-aged English woman. Being part of a professional theatre production, performing in front of a live audience, was an exhilarating leap into the world I had always dreamed of.

I thoroughly enjoyed organising events to raise money for William Bates Academy and Theatre. During one such fundraiser, I met the charismatic frontman of Rabbit, an Australian rock band. Surprisingly, he asked me out, and I accepted. He was not only the frontman of this band but also the original singer of AC/DC. He cooked dinner for me and introduced me to the music of Pavarotti, amused that I hadn't explored opera, despite my Italian heritage. However, my musical tastes had only recently expanded to include operettas, thanks to William's friendship with Suzanne Steele, an acclaimed opera singer who was a regular guest at our fundraisers due to her popularity.

Life at this time was exhilarating. I hardly spent any time at home, choosing instead to immerse myself in work, frequent nightclubs, and attend theatre shows—anything to keep away from the oppressive environment at home. Unfortunately, my father continued to seize every opportunity to inflict physical harm. At 23, I reached my breaking point. After a particularly severe incident, I declared it was the last time he would hit me—I was leaving for good. He coldly stated that if I left, I could never return, and I could only take what I could gather in thirty minutes. Determined, I packed my car with a few essential belongings, including my clothes, photo albums, and music collections, and left.

I found refuge in Glen Iris with friends who had previously offered support. They had two young boys I occasionally babysat, providing a sense of family and normalcy. It was with them that I first truly opened up about the abuse at home. They were incredibly supportive, and their 93-year-old uncle generously lent me the money for a bond on a one-bedroom unit in Malvern. I moved in, borrowing some furniture temporarily, embracing the independence, though initially anxious about living on my own.

Despite my departure, I continued visiting my mother, facing my father's hostility during each visit. He demanded I leave, but I stood my ground, reminding him that it was as much my mother's home as his. Over the next six months, his attitude softened, and he begrudgingly accepted my presence without further argument.

One memorable evening, the friends who had taken me in asked if I could accompany their 93-year-old uncle to a function since they were unavailable. I agreed, assuming the event would last only a couple of hours, given his age. However, we were the first to arrive and the last to leave—he relished having a young woman on his arm, proudly introducing me to his friends, many of whom were his old war buddies. The evening was unexpectedly enjoyable, filled with engaging stories and camaraderie.

Afterwards, as I drove him home and bid him goodbye with a peck on the cheek, his playful jest about my modest farewell caught me off guard. I laughed it off, a reminder of the timeless nature of charm and flirtation.

Despite enjoying these new experiences, I found myself tired of the constant uncertainty and rejection from countless auditions. Choosing not to endure the financial struggles my parents faced, I decided against pursuing a professional acting career and instead began promotional work, which offered more stability and less stress.

While working as an Aramis brand ambassador at Myer, I met a young man of colour who quickly became a significant part of my life. Initially, I was hesitant to date someone younger, but he misled me about his age, claiming to be older. It wasn't until his mother called to invite me to his 21st birthday that I discovered the truth. Though upset, the bond we had formed was strong enough to continue our relationship.

Eventually, we decided to move in together, buying a unit without announcing our cohabitation. While his family was aware since he had been living at home, my parents were kept in the dark, or so I believed. Our relationship progressed to an engagement, celebrated with a large party at my parents' home attended by about 150 guests, where I had my best friend as my maid of honour.

Looking back, I realise that I made many mistakes in navigating my first serious relationship. I had a habit of involving my best friend in everything I did with my boyfriend, turning most of our dates into a trio. This dynamic, however, began to shift, and I noticed her visiting my fiancé when I was away and reducing her communication with me. Concerns from his family about their closeness prompted a tearful confrontation, but both denied any romantic involvement. Despite this, our relationship continued to deteriorate, leading to the eventual cancellation of our wedding. This difficult period taught me profound lessons about trust, relationships, and self-awareness.

My ex-fiancé and I found ourselves in a constant cycle of breakups and reconciliations, a situation that left us both emotionally drained. Understanding that one of us needed to make a significant change to break this cycle, I decided it would be me. Despite his frequent talks of travelling, I knew he lacked the resolve to make such a drastic decision. Thus, I planned to move overseas, giving myself a window of two to five years abroad to truly distance myself and gain perspective.

A friend, sharing my desire for change, decided to join me, and together we planned our journey. I hoped to keep our jointly owned unit as an investment, a fallback plan to return to. However, my ex-fiancé initially resisted this idea, leading us to put the unit up for sale. On the very day I was set to leave, I felt a pang of hope; if he had asked me to stay and work things out, I would have cancelled my trip. But instead of making that request, he came to my parents' house to say goodbye, a gesture that was poignant yet too late to change my plans.

Instead, as I arrived in Singapore, he called to express his regret and newfound agreement on keeping the unit. During the call, he mentioned how much he missed me and expressed his desire to catch up in London. By then, however, we had already signed the contract to sell the unit. We agreed that if it didn't sell at the asking price, we would keep it, but fate decided otherwise—it sold.

Travelling through Singapore and Malaysia marked my first international adventure, and I embraced every moment. From tourist attractions to a charming little village in Malaysia introduced by a local, the experiences enriched me. The people's warmth contrasted starkly with a harrowing incident in Singapore. It was 1987, a tense time following the execution of two Australians for drug trafficking. As my friend and I made frequent trips in and out of Singapore, our final departure for London raised suspicions at customs. The fear that her new English acquaintance might have planted drugs in her luggage loomed over us, but fortunately, the officers found nothing more incriminating than boxes of tampons—a discovery that seemed to embarrass them more than us.

After a cramped and chaotic flight, where passengers were herded like sardines, and some were even seated in the aisles due to overbooking, my friend and I finally touched down in London. Our excitement was palpable, yet it quickly dimmed upon reaching our hotel. Having spent a substantial amount for what we hoped would be a luxurious accommodation akin to our opulent stay in Singapore, we were met with a stark contrast. The room was minuscule, more akin to a cupboard than a place to rest. Stepping out of the bed meant practically stepping into the shower, and the space was so confined it barely accommodated our luggage, let alone allowed any room to manoeuvre.

Determined not to let our cramped quarters dampen our spirits, we spent the next five days exploring the city as extensively as possible. Each day was packed with sightseeing, immersing ourselves in the rich tapestry of London's culture and history. Amidst our explorations, we also embarked on a mission to find a more suitable means of continuing our European adventure. Eventually, our efforts paid off when we stumbled upon a camper van, which felt like a treasure amidst our logistical challenges. For eight hundred pounds, we acquired our new travel companion, thrilled by the prospect of the freedom it promised. This van was not just a vehicle; it was our ticket to roam across Europe, promising a journey filled with new landscapes and uncharted experiences.

The phone call from my ex-fiancé came, but it wasn't to coordinate our reunion in London as I had hoped. Instead, he confessed that he had met someone else and decided to pursue a new relationship. I was utterly stunned. Just a week after leaving, his profession of missing me had been replaced by a new affection. I felt betrayed and foolish for holding on to his previous words. The realisation that I had wasted so much time and emotion on him left me seething with frustration at myself.

Determined to move forward, my friend and I set off for Dover on a crisp Sunday afternoon. Our plan was to catch the ferry to Calais the following morning. Upon our arrival in Dover, my wonderfully ditzy friend managed to lock the keys inside the van. Left with no other choice, we had to enlist the help of a local to break into our own vehicle—a slightly embarrassing but necessary action. Unfortunately, the typically breathtaking view of the White Cliffs of Dover was obscured by a dense fog that day, and apparently every other day, diminishing the scenic experience we had anticipated.

Upon crossing into Calais, I relinquished the driving responsibilities to my friend, hesitant to navigate on the 'wrong' side of the road. We arrived in Calais on a Monday afternoon with the immediate plan to exchange our money at the local bank. Unfortunately, we discovered that banks in Calais are closed on Monday afternoons, leaving us momentarily stranded without local currency.

As we delved deeper into France, the enchanting charm of the small towns captivated us. Each town appeared as if plucked from a postcard, with their quaint beauty further enhancing the magic of our journey. The French people proved incredibly welcoming; their friendliness was particularly evident when we made attempts to speak French. Even our clumsiest attempts were met with nothing but helpfulness and encouragement, transforming each

34

interaction into delightful cultural exchanges that enriched our travel experience.

Driven by growing hunger and with limited payment options, we eventually stopped at a small café. Regrettably, our various forms of currency were not accepted there. Remarkably, the café owner, upon hearing of our predicament, generously allowed us to dine on whatever we liked, trusting that we would return the next day to settle the bill. He expressed a particular fondness for Australians, confident in our trustworthiness.

Grateful for his kindness, we spent the remainder of the day exploring the picturesque village. That night, we returned to the comfort of our camper van for a restful sleep, recharging for the adventures ahead. The next morning, we promptly visited the bank as soon as it opened, exchanged our money, and returned to the café to thank the owner personally and pay for our meals. His unwavering trust and hospitality were profoundly touching, reinforcing the goodness and warmth we found so far from home and igniting my newfound appreciation for the French culture and its people.

As we continued our European adventure, our route took us through the scenic vistas of France, Germany, and Switzerland. Driving through the Swiss Alps was so magical, with white snow and quaint chalets—it was spectacular. We even stopped at one of the chalets to have a drink. It was extremely expensive, but the place was cosy. My friend requested that they light up a candle at our table so we could take photos. I am sure the waiter thought we were a gay couple.

We had to go through so many checkpoints along the way. We spent the evening in Geneva, and the city was breathtakingly beautiful, with the lights shimmering over Lake Geneva.

However, an unforgettable incident unfolded in Geneva that tested our resolve. Desperate to find parking in a city where luxury cars are the norm, we inadvertently drove our camper van into an underground car park. It soon became apparent that the height of our van exceeded the clearance limit, trapping us in a precarious position where we could neither advance further into the garage nor reverse out.

The situation behind us quickly escalated, with a line of cars eager to park. The driver in the sleek black Mercedes directly behind us started honking his horn incessantly, his impatience mounting by the minute. In an attempt to defuse the tension, I stepped out of the van and approached him, hoping to explain our predicament and possibly collaborate on a solution. Despite my attempts to communicate using my high school French, the interaction deteriorated rapidly. The driver's demeanour was far from the graciousness often attributed to the French; instead, his overt arrogance and rudeness became apparent, revealing his German-French heritage, which might have contributed to his scant patience for what he perceived as a trivial delay caused by two women in an outdated van. He even audaciously suggested that Australians should invest in better cars and learn proper driving—a comment that seemed irrelevant given the circumstances with our van's height.

Inside the van, my friend, following his aggressive directives to navigate across the centre lane, narrowly avoided a head-on collision with another Mercedes by mere centimetres. We found ourselves in a tense game of musical chairs in the driving seat, each taking turns attempting to navigate out of the predicament.

After about thirty minutes of careful manoeuvring and sheer determination, we finally freed our van from the confines of Geneva's underground car park labyrinth. This exhausting ordeal left us not only tired but also enlightened about the complexities of driving in foreign urban environments, especially in a vehicle not designed for such tight spaces.

Driving through the Mont Blanc Tunnel was an exhilarating yet unsettling experience, given my claustrophobia. The tunnel seemed endless, but emerging into Italy, the view was nothing short of breathtaking—a vision that felt like a once-in-a-lifetime revelation. However, descending from the majestic mountains, the initial impression of Italy was underwhelming. The buildings appeared old, dirty, and dilapidated, starkly contrasting the charming villages of France and Switzerland we had passed through. Our route meandered through Aoste, Torino, Asti, and finally, Genoa.

My friend's displeasure with Italy began the moment she set foot there, colouring our journey with her constant complaints. The narrow, steep, and winding roads leading to Genoa did little to ease the tension, particularly terrifying when faced with oncoming traffic. Her frustrations peaked, and she expressed a desire to return to London or even Australia.

Our challenges compounded when we reached Pisa; my friend's worsening condition rushed us to the hospital, where she was diagnosed with appendicitis and required immediate surgery. In Italian hospitals, where nurses are not accustomed to extensive bedside care, I found myself thrust into the role of nursemaid. Thankfully, the kindness of several locals in Pisa provided support and made the ordeal manageable.

While my days were consumed with caregiving, the evenings allowed me some respite to explore the historical city. It was in Pisa that I experienced my first taste of Tiramisu. Even though I was sceptical at first, the waiter assured me that if I didn't enjoy it, I wouldn't have to pay. Not only did I gladly pay for it, but I also indulged in a second serving. That delectable dessert marked the beginning of my enduring love affair with Tiramisu, a sweet highlight in an otherwise tumultuous leg of our journey.

Amidst the quaint charm of Pisa, I found myself grappling with a deep sense of loneliness, missing the familiarity of home more acutely than ever. The midday closures of shops from 1:00 p.m. to 4:00 p.m. were a stark reminder of the cultural differences that I struggled to adapt to, leaving me feeling disconnected during those long afternoons.

As I stood before the Leaning Tower of Pisa, I was simultaneously enchanted by its storied slant and a touch disappointed; it was shorter than I had imagined. Despite this, the rich history of the tower captivated my interest, providing a complex mix of awe and a subtle sense of letdown that mirrored my emotional state during this leg of my journey.

The release of my friend from the hospital presented us with a new challenge. She was eager to return to Australia, hoping to fly out from Rome. However, the doctors advised against flying immediately, recommending a week's recuperation instead. Faced with this unforeseen delay, I reached out to family friends living in Pisciotta, a small town in Salerno not far from Palinuro, hoping they could host us during her recovery. I hadn't seen these friends since leaving Italy 18 years ago.

Pisciotta is nestled in the stunning landscape of the Cilento coast, a prized stretch between the Gulf of Salerno and the Gulf of Policastro, famed for its Blue Flag beaches and as one of Campania's most breathtaking coastlines. My hope was that the serene environment and warm hospitality would persuade my friend to continue our journey, at least until we returned to London. I was apprehensive about the prospect of manoeuvring the camper van alone across Europe.

Thankfully, our friends in Pisciotta welcomed us with open arms, generously offering to host us for as long as needed. The journey to Pisciotta was an adventure in itself, characterised by a winding ascent up steep hills on narrow roads—a challenging yet picturesque drive that led us to a haven of tranquillity and friendship.

Upon arriving in Pisciotta, I navigated the camper to the town centre, parking it there because the streets leading to my friends' house were exceedingly narrow—so constricted that we had to sidle along sideways with our luggage to reach their home.

The house itself was charming, with a living area that opened onto a balcony boasting a stunning view of the ocean. The first time I stepped onto the balcony, I was taken aback by the sheer drop; it jutted out over a rugged cliff directly above the sea. My fear of heights instantly kicked in, making me apprehensive to linger too close to the edge, despite the breathtaking view.

During our week in Pisciotta, my Italian friend took us frequently to visit Marina di Pisciotta, a charming coastal area just a few kilometres away. This little town is a picturesque tourist port, where one can witness spectacular sunsets or gaze out over the deep blue of the horizon. We handled our shopping and banking needs there, soaking up the vibrant local atmosphere. I hoped that this beautiful side of Italy would encourage my friend to reconsider and stay longer. However, despite the allure of the coast and the warmth of the Italian hospitality, she decided to return to Rome after a week to fly back to Australia.

This left me to navigate Italy and the journey back to London on my own. I was not just disappointed but also frightened; I had never before travelled alone, not even within Australia, let alone in a distant foreign country. The prospect of continuing the adventure without the security of a companion was daunting, stirring a mix of anticipation and apprehension within me.

As the camper van pulled away from the scenic shores of Pisciotta, I felt a mix of emotions. The departure of my friend marked the end of an era of companionship and shared discoveries, leaving me to face the winding roads ahead alone. This journey had transformed me from a companion on a shared adventure into a solitary traveller, poised at the edge of new experiences and personal growth.

Despite my trepidation, there was an undercurrent of excitement. The road ahead was mine to explore, filled with opportunities to forge my path and meet the challenges head-on. I had already navigated foreign lands and unexpected situations; now, it was time to discover what I could do on my own.

As I drove away, the fading lights of Pisciotta behind me and the vast, starlit sky above, I realised that my story was far from over. The next chapter awaited, ready to be written with the lessons learned from the past and the dreams of what was yet to come.

Chapter 5

Return to Roots

Leaving Pisciotta was bittersweet. The van, once shared, was now mine alone to steer. As I navigated the familiar yet distant roads of Italy, I felt a profound pull towards my past. My next destination was Calabria, a region that held the echoes of my childhood and the memories of family long not seen. It was here that I would reconnect with my heritage, revisit the old homestead, and meet relatives who were integral threads in the fabric of my identity.

Each kilometre brought me closer to my ancestral home, and with each passing landscape, I found pieces of my heart that I had left behind. The journey was more than a physical traverse across Italy; it was a pilgrimage to the roots that had shaped me.

As the picturesque landscapes of Italy unfolded before me, my journey took me to San Gregorio D'Ippona, a quaint town perched between the verdant valleys of the Mesima River and the gentle slopes of Mount Poro. This town, where ancient Greece once whispered its secrets into the Italian ethos through the colony of Hipponion, was now a humble commune dedicated to the age-old art of olive oil production. The extra virgin olive oil here, lauded for its purity, is drawn from the olives that thrive in the abundant sunlight, thanks to the town's lofty hilltop perch.

Here, in this serene setting, I stayed with my mother's only surviving brother, immersing myself in family connections, new and old. Some cousins were just faint memories from my childhood, while others were faces I was seeing for the first time. Reconnecting with them was heartwarming, yet the slow pace of life in such a small town had its limits—each day was a routine of visiting from one home to another, a repetition of walls and familial stories.

The restrictions of local customs were palpable. My young female cousin, for instance, could only join me on outings if accompanied by her brother, reflecting the protective norms still prevalent in rural Italian cultures. One day, seizing a chance for a bit of independence, I invited her to visit Calimera, my birthplace. The permission granted for a daytime adventure allowed us a brief escape from the watchful eyes of tradition.

Driving through the familiar yet distant streets of Calimera was a surreal experience. The town had shrunk significantly since my childhood, from a bustling community of 1,500 to a quiet gathering of over 600. Most of the shops had disappeared, replaced by a solitary bar—a last refuge for the town's elderly to reminisce and pass the time.

Revisiting my old school and the houses of my neighbours stirred a mix of nostalgia and pain. Each corner of Calimera echoed with the ghosts of my past, the shadows of my father's harsh discipline darkening the sunlit streets. As I met with relatives and old friends, it seemed all they wanted to do was remind me of these past hardships, unintentionally reviving memories I had struggled to set aside. Although the town was filled with relatives eager to host me, their well-meaning invitations only deepened the weight of old memories, making the prospect daunting. I made polite promises to return, but inside, my heart was heavy with the burden of past hurts.

The journey continued to San Calogero, where my maternal grandfather, at the venerable age of 89, still maintained his independence living alone. As dusk approached, he insisted on accompanying us back, his presence a supposed shield against the unpredictable night. Our drive took us through Mileto during a street festival, where the vibrant energy of youth contrasted sharply with my grandfather's protective stance. His concern, though touching, was a poignant reminder of the generational divides that shaped our perceptions of safety and adventure.

That evening, as we navigated the festive crowds and the winding roads back to San Gregorio, I pondered the complex tapestry of fear and freedom, tradition, and change. My journey through Italy was more than a simple visit; it was an exploration of the ties that bind us to our past and the personal growth that comes from stepping beyond them.

Eager to expand my horizons beyond the quaint towns of Calabria, I seized an opportunity to travel to Sicily when my mother's cousin invited me to stay with them in Messina. He was caretaking the Caserma situated in the picturesque Piazza del Duomo, providing a perfect base from which to explore the vibrant culture and flavours of Sicily.

Each morning began with a delightful ritual: Stepping out to greet the day, I was greeted in turn by the enticing aroma of freshly brewed coffee from a nearby cart. Here, I indulged in the most delicious granita al caffè con panna, savouring three of these icy treats each morning along with a sweet, crisp cannoli. My sweet tooth was thoroughly spoilt in this corner of Italy, where culinary delights beckoned at every turn.

My cousins, eager to show off the beauty of their homeland, took me on excursions to some of Sicily's most breathtaking locales. We ventured to Taormina, a stunning hilltop town on the east coast, near the formidable Mount Etna. This active volcano, which had recently erupted, added a thrilling backdrop to our visits. Taormina charmed me with its ancient Greco-Roman theatre, the Teatro Antico di Taormina, which is still a hub of cultural activity today.

We also explored other intriguing sites like Milazzo and Tindari, home to the revered statue of the Black Madonna. I was fascinated by the legend of this Byzantine icon, which is said to have been smuggled from Constantinople during the eighth and ninth centuries. According to local lore, a storm forced sailors to offload the statue at the port of Tindari, where it has been venerated ever since.

Perhaps the most memorable experience was walking on the recent ash deposits of Mount Etna. The ground underfoot was still warm, the air filled with a smoky haze. The ash painted my feet and legs black, marking me as a traveller who had literally walked through fire.

This chapter of my journey was not just about sightseeing; it was a deeper exploration into the rich tapestry of Sicilian life and the enduring bonds of family. Despite the allure of Sicily's landscapes and legends, it was the simple moments of sharing granita with friendly faces that truly encapsulated the spirit of my Sicilian sojourn.

After spending the most idyllic months in Sicily, I reluctantly left its enchanting embrace to return to Calabria. Despite the geographical change, the pace of life remained unchanged, steeped in the familiar rhythms of small-town existence. One day, a surprising invitation came from my young cousin's fiancé, who offered to take me out for a day while the others were occupied. Eager for a diversion, I accepted, unaware of his true intentions.

He drove us to a secluded beach, where the solitude was unsettling rather than romantic. As we walked along the shore, he abruptly confessed his desire to make love to me. I was shocked, to say the least. Not only was he engaged to my cousin, but he was also far from my type. I confronted him, incredulous at his audacity, reminding him of his commitment to my cousin. His dismissive response, suggesting that 'she didn't need to know,' chilled me to the bone. From that moment on, I made sure never to find myself alone with him again. His willingness to betray so close to home made me question what he might be capable of with others, casting a shadow over my trust.

This unsettling encounter marked a stark contrast to the warmth and beauty I had experienced in Sicily, reminding me of the complex, sometimes dark, nature of human relationships. The incident lingered in my thoughts as I continued navigating the familial and social landscapes of Calabria, now with a more cautious heart.

After a three-month stay in Calabria, I ventured northward, traversing the eastern coastline of Italy. My journey led me through Puglia and several other regions, each a brief but vivid chapter in my travels. My destination was Mariano Comense, a small town nestled between Como and Milan, where my mother's only surviving sister resided. I was hopeful that the northern cities would offer the vibrant life I craved, a stark contrast to the slow-paced south.

Milan initially didn't live up to my expectations of a bustling major city; it appeared somewhat bland at first glance. However, as I delved deeper into its streets and culture, the city began to reveal its charms. There was an abundance to see and do, and gradually, I found myself enamoured with its hidden vibrancy.

Como, with its stunning vistas and serene lake, initially mesmerised me with its visual splendour. However, after a few days, the scenic tranquillity began to feel monotonous. I have always thrived on activity and energy, and Como's quietude soon lacked the excitement I sought. In contrast, Milan offered the dynamism I craved. The city captivated me with its lively narrative and vibrant culture, quickly becoming a place I not only appreciated but grew to love.

As a prime tourist destination, Como is especially popular with Swiss, French, and German visitors during the summer months. Their presence infuses the town with a bustling, international vibe, contributing to a lively nightlife scene filled with piano bars and upscale venues. Yet, this comes at a high cost; in 1987, the price for a simple drink could escalate to about six thousand liras—a substantial amount at that time. Bars often required the purchase of a drink, making even casual outings expensive.

Additionally, many of these bars chose American music over traditional Italian melodies, somewhat diluting the local charm I had hoped to find. This musical shift, while potentially appealing to international tourists, left much to be desired for those like myself, eager to immerse in the authentic Italian cultural experience.

While staying with my aunt and her family in Mariano Comense, I became acquainted with one of my cousin's girlfriends. She was a delightful person, though it was clear that my cousin was not as invested in the relationship as she was; he was involved with another girl at the time. Despite the complicated romantic dynamics, she graciously took me under her wing, and we spent most nights exploring Milan's vibrant nightlife.

My aunt, understanding my need for independence, usually left the front door of the apartment unlocked, so I could come and go as I pleased. This arrangement worked perfectly until one night when things didn't go as planned. After an exhilarating evening at a gay nightclub in Milan, we returned home around 2:00 a.m.. She dropped me off and continued on her way. To my surprise, I found the front door locked. Unsure of what to do and not wanting to disturb anyone, I knocked softly, hoping someone would hear. But as the minutes ticked by on those cold marble steps, no one came.

Eventually, I gave up waiting and started walking the quiet, dark streets of Mariano Comense. Aimlessly wandering, I ended up in the town centre, where I spotted my friend's car. To my relief, it was unlocked. Exhausted, I climbed into the back seat and fell asleep.

The next morning, my friend found me there, startled but amused at my predicament. After explaining what had happened, she questioned why I hadn't just come to her apartment. However, given the typical Italian apartment setups with large, imposing doors, I hadn't wanted to ring her bell and risk waking her. It was one of those unexpected adventures that added a touch of surreal humour to my Italian experiences.

While in Milan, I also had the opportunity to meet my childhood pen pal from Mantova. For years, we had exchanged letters but had never met in person. Accompanied by my new friend and another companion, I was finally able to meet her, her husband, and their baby girl. It was a delight to connect with someone I had known through words alone for so long. We spent a wonderful day together, catching up and sharing stories face-to-face.

A few weeks later, I returned to spend a weekend with them. They kindly showed me around, taking me to see various local sights, including the beautiful Lago di Garda. During our visit, they shared how the area was increasingly being bought up by German investors, a trend that was both impressive and somewhat disheartening. The influence of money in reshaping these quaint towns was palpable, highlighting the changes sweeping through even the most historic places.

Finally, the moment arrived for me to visit Venice, a city that had long been etched on my must-see list. I had heard various stories about Venice being smelly, dirty, and prohibitively expensive, which had somewhat tempered my expectations. However, upon arrival, I was pleasantly surprised to find none of these rumours to be true. The city was neither dirty nor smelly; perhaps this was due to the cleaning efforts in anticipation of the 13th G7 Summit, which hosted leaders from around the world. Since that first visit, I've returned to Venice several times and have consistently found it to be a charming and clean place. It seems that the complaints I had heard were greatly exaggerated, or perhaps I just saw the city in a different light.

After spending a few enriching months in Milan, I began to yearn for the familiarity of the English language. Living in Italy, I noticed that I was starting to forget certain English words, which added a layer of frustration to my daily life. The desire to hear and speak English fluently again grew stronger by the day, compelling me to decide to leave Italy.

Despite my longing to return to London, I deeply cherished the time spent with my cousins in northern Italy. I promised my cousin that I would return to be the best man at his wedding, a commitment I was eager to fulfil. Around the same time, my newly made friend expressed a desire to visit London as well. Given that I had to drive the camper van back alone, her company was not only welcome for the companionship but also practical, as it allowed us to split the steep petrol costs. This arrangement worked out perfectly, blending the need for a familiar company with the practicalities of a long drive across Europe.

Embarking on our journey back to London, my newfound friend and I tackled the long drive with few stops, only pausing to stretch our legs and catch some sleep. Upon our arrival in London, we temporarily settled in a hotel for a few nights. Fortunately, a relative of an Australian friend graciously hosted us while I began the daunting task of searching for a rental place.

The quest for accommodation in London proved challenging. The rental market was not only expensive but also disheartening. I recall one particularly distressing viewing: As soon as I opened the gate to the property, I was overwhelmed. Although I have a fondness for cats, the number of them around the property wasn't the issue—it was the unbearable stench, and the unsightly mess they left behind that made me physically ill. This experience was one of many hurdles as I navigated the competitive and often disheartening housing market in London.

Upon my return to London, I was greeted by a couple of letters from my original travel companion from Australia. They were waiting for me in my post office box, containing her requests for a refund of her 50 per cent share of the van and for the return of her belongings. Her demands took me by surprise and left a sour taste, given that I had shouldered all the travel and maintenance expenses by myself throughout our time in Italy.

Feeling a mix of frustration and obligation, I responded to her. I explained that the proceeds from the van's sale would first cover the outstanding costs I had incurred. Only then could I consider refunding any remaining funds. I also assured her that I would ship her belongings back, but that the cost of postage would be deducted from her share of the van's sale. Her persistent inquiries about the financial settlement continued to be a point of contention between us.

Navigating the challenges of settling in London, I found myself simultaneously hunting for a place to live, seeking employment, and attempting to sell the van—a daunting trifecta. After an exhaustive search, I finally secured a room in a shared house in Ealing. The space was incredibly compact, and the rent was steep, comparable to what one might pay for a one-bedroom apartment in Malvern, an affluent suburb of Melbourne. Despite the high cost and limited space, it was one of the better accommodations available, and I had no choice but to make it work.

The bay window in my room was repurposed as my dressing table, providing a much-needed personal touch. Although the wardrobe was small, it sufficed, and thankfully, the house was clean. My housemates included one other woman and two men, all of whom were pleasant enough. The communal aspect of our living arrangement turned out to be quite bearable, and I've even kept in touch with one of my roommates to this day.

The van found a temporary resting place just up the street from my new home, as parking proved to be yet another challenge in London. Amidst these adjustments, I secured a position as a payroll assistant at TSB, which was the fifth-largest bank in the UK at the time. My boss, a Scotsman, was difficult to understand at first, but I found his demeanour quite entertaining. He bore an uncanny resemblance to Basil Fawlty from *Fawlty Towers*, not only in looks but in his mannerisms as well. Unfortunately, our sizable office was shared with a third colleague—a lovely man but one whose personal hygiene was noticeably lacking, to put it mildly. In this new setting, I quickly became known as the 'Brash Australian' among my coworkers.

One evening after work, one of my housemates caught me off guard with a question about the van. His casual inquiry, 'Have you sold the van?' seemed odd, prompting me to ask why he would think that. He revealed that he had seen someone driving it away earlier that day. My heart sank as the realisation hit me: The van had been stolen. I immediately contacted the police, but they were not optimistic, suggesting it was likely taken apart for parts by now.

After the van theft, the insurance company provided a modest reimbursement. With those funds, I managed to return the personal belongings to my friend in Australia and continued my employment at TSB Bank. During this period, I started a relationship with another man of colour. My friends in Australia felt he bore a resemblance to my ex-fiancé, a comparison I either did not see or chose to ignore. He was genuinely kind-hearted, yet he was cautious about fully committing to our relationship, aware of my longing to return home. I later started dating an Englishman I met at the bank.

After six months at the bank, I grew restless; the job offered little challenge. I seized an opportunity to work at an engineering firm in Putney, where I reported to a wonderful female boss. The dynamic in this smaller office was invigorating, as it was just the two of us managing the operations.

Around the same time, I moved out of my shared house in Ealing and into an apartment in Southfields that my new boyfriend had recently purchased. The rent was equivalent to what I had been paying in Ealing. This move marked yet another chapter in my journey, blending professional growth with personal transitions, each step moving me closer to realising where and how I wanted to build my future.

After a year together, my boyfriend proposed. Despite the deep connection we had fostered, I hesitated. My heart longed for Australia—its vast landscapes and the familiarity of home were calling me back. Each time he brought up marriage, I found myself evading the commitment, not ready to settle down.

Understanding my reluctance yet eagerness to compromise, he suggested a plan that seemed like a middle ground: We would move to Hong Kong for a few years before ultimately relocating to Australia. Reluctantly, I agreed, hoping this could be a step toward fulfilling both our desires.

Nearly two years after leaving Australia, we returned so he could meet my family and finalise preparations for our move to Hong Kong. He had successfully secured a position with the Bank of Hong Kong, and everything seemed to be aligning for him. However, as I greeted him at the airport, a stark realisation washed over me—I didn't love him as he deserved to be loved, nor did I yearn to join him on this new adventure.

Amidst the festive cheer of Christmas, I struggled with my feelings, not wanting to dampen the holiday spirit. The family decided to dine out for Christmas lunch, a pleasant distraction, but the day ended abruptly with a car accident. Someone ran a red light and collided with the front of our car. I seized on this incident, hoping to avoid further travel, but we continued our journey to Adelaide as planned.

In Adelaide, I found the courage to express my true feelings. It was heart-wrenching to end the relationship, especially knowing he had moved away from his family to be with me. He was understandably upset, his plans and sacrifices crumbling before him. This breakup, though painful, was the kindest decision I could make, freeing both of us from a future that wasn't meant to be.

While my ex-boyfriend settled in Hong Kong, he found love with a wonderful English woman. They married and had a son, and by all accounts, he found the happiness he deserved. This turn of events prompted me to introspect deeply about my own hesitations in relationships. Growing up, I had witnessed Italian men who often treated their wives more like housemaids than partners, and the prevalence of domestic violence left a deep imprint on me. These experiences, combined with a general mistrust of men, significantly shaped my views on relationships and commitment.

As I reflected on my journey, I recognised that my past had shaped not just my fears but also my strengths. The experiences I had navigated—from the vibrant streets of Milan to the complex dynamics of relationships—had taught me much about resilience and self-awareness. Each relationship, each farewell, had been a stepping stone towards understanding my own needs and boundaries more clearly.

With these reflections, I turned my gaze forward, ready to confront and embrace the next phase of my life. The following chapter would find me delving deeper into personal healing, seeking to understand the roots of my hesitations in relationships and striving for a future where I could love freely and fully, unencumbered by the shadows of the past.

Chapter 6

From Surviving to Thriving

Back in Melbourne, the skyline welcomed me like a familiar embrace, yet I returned a changed person, shaped by my experiences abroad. As I resettled into the city's rhythm, I found comfort in the predictability of office work, a stark contrast to the adventurous life I had briefly led for almost two years. However, it was my engagement with local charities that truly rekindled my spirit and purpose. This chapter of my life became a testament to giving back, leveraging my skills and experiences to support community causes that touched my heart deeply.

From organising fundraisers to participating in direct aid, I immersed myself in efforts to combat the AIDS crisis that had taken a toll on many friends in the 1980s and to support the arts community, which had always been a sanctuary for me. This period wasn't just about professional and personal recovery; it was about making meaningful contributions, using my renewed energy to make a difference in the lives of others and reconnecting with the community that had shaped me.

My return also marked a new phase in family relationships. Recognising my need for independence, my parents had built a room for me at the back of our family home, providing the privacy I craved. My relationship with my father, once marked by harsh discipline, had softened with distance and time. Though the physical abuse had ceased, the emotional scars remained, creating a complex tapestry of forgiveness, understanding, and silent acknowledgment of our shared past.

In this new chapter at home, I strived not only to heal but to thrive, channelling my energies into impactful work and rebuilding connections with a deeper appreciation of my roots and the person I had become.

In 1992, after three years of working in payroll and HR, my yearning for independence led me to start my own venture. With a solid background in figures and administration, I launched a bookkeeping and payroll administration service. At that time, the market for such services was largely underserved, with most firms opting for in-house staff or large bureaus. Recognising this gap, I began actively marketing my business.

The response was overwhelming. Within a year, I was working non-stop—24 hours a day, seven days a week. The business was not just surviving; it was thriving, providing me with a decent living. By 1994, bolstered by my success and the need for more hands, I bought a house with my sister, who assisted with data entry in my business. As the business grew, so did my reputation for quality and reliability.

For relaxation, my sister and I developed a weekly routine of visiting the newly opened casino in 1994. We would each gamble a modest $50, satisfied with any winnings, even if it was just a few hundred dollars. These outings, however, were less about gambling and more about taking a much-needed break to relax and socialise after long hours at work.

Despite the intense workload, I still maintained my commitment to charity and volunteering work, a testament to my dedication to giving back to the community despite the demands of my time. One of my enjoyments was volunteering to assist at the Victorian Arts Centre. Although I was no longer working in the industry, I still had a great love for live theatre.

In 1994, during my time volunteering at the Arts Centre, I had the serendipitous encounter that would lead me to meet my future husband at the age of 38. I was drafted to assist with one of their gala fundraising dinners—an evening dedicated to raising funds for the centre. David, who was the Business Manager at the Arts Centre at the time, was instrumental in that event. We worked well together, enjoyed a successful evening, and raised a significant amount of money. However, it wasn't until a year later, in 1995, that our paths crossed again when David contacted me to help with another fundraising event. Despite the short notice—only a couple of weeks before the event—I agreed to assist, though my social life had been largely eclipsed by my business commitments.

The event was another triumph, fun-filled and lucrative. The next day, we reconvened for a debriefing at the Sofitel, and after the formal discussion, David and I lingered to chat. During our conversation, I mentioned that I had inquired about tickets to see the film adaptation of Shakespeare's *Othello*. To my surprise, David offered to secure the tickets for me. Gratefully, I accepted, thinking nothing more of it until a call the next day clarified that David had assumed we would attend together. Caught off guard but not wanting to disappoint, I agreed to join him.

Our date was set for a Sunday; David would pick me up at 9:00 a.m. for breakfast before the movie at 11:00 a.m.. I faced a minor wardrobe dilemma, as my attire was predominantly formal due to my work. Wanting to strike the right balance, I purchased and tailored a pair of jeans specifically for the occasion. When David arrived to pick me up, it was clear he was suffering the effects of the previous night's festivities—a housewarming party had left him rather worse for wear.

We went to a café for breakfast, one of my clients, where David could only muster the appetite for some unbuttered toast, which he barely touched. Concerned, my client checked if there was an issue with the food, prompting me to explain his condition discreetly.

The movie session itself was somewhat disjointed; David spent much of it in and out of the bathroom, leaving me to watch *Othello* mostly by myself. Despite the awkward start, we spent a pleasant afternoon back at my place, just talking and watching TV, easing into a comfortable camaraderie.

The next day brought an unexpected gesture that touched my heart—a beautiful bouquet of flowers and a box of chocolates left at my doorstep. Just as I was admiring them, David called to ensure they had been delivered. His timing was perfect, and his choice of florist was impeccable. He inquired about my evening plans, and upon hearing of my modest dinner plans with my sister—a roast I was nervously preparing—I invited him to join us. He accepted, grateful for the company and perhaps eager to strengthen the budding connection between us. That evening, as we shared a simple meal, the foundations of a deeper relationship were laid, marked by thoughtful gestures, shared laughter, and the warmth of family hospitality.

David and I quickly became inseparable, yet navigating our cultural differences brought both challenges and amusing moments. Despite his employment at the Arts Centre, David, an Aussie from the country, was still adjusting to the nuances of Italian culture. One of my cherished rituals was a morning visit to Brunetti in Carlton for an espresso and a pastry—a tradition steeped in my Italian heritage.

On his first outing with me to Brunetti, David innocently ordered a caffe latte and carrot cake. I paused, a smile tugging at my lips, and gently explained, 'Do you realise where we are? This isn't just any café; it's an Italian institution, and no, they don't serve carrot cake here—that's very Australian.' He looked genuinely surprised, not only by the absence of carrot cake but also by my preference for boldly flavoured espresso, sweetened with sugar.

This small culinary misstep highlighted the delightful contrasts between our backgrounds. It became a recurring joke between us, emblematic of our journey to blend his Australian ways with my Italian traditions. Each such instance brought us closer, infusing our relationship with a sense of warmth and shared humour over the simple things that could so easily set us apart.

In May 1995, while my parents were away on a three-month trip to Italy, my relationship with David began to blossom. Taking advantage of their absence, David and I sneaked away for a holiday to Hamilton Island, a getaway that remained a secret from my parents. During this time, David grew close to my siblings and even received an invitation to my nephew's baptism, scheduled soon after my parents' return.

Faced with the dilemma of introducing David to my parents on the day of the christening—a situation I wanted to avoid—I decided to organise a more intimate setting. I hosted a dinner at my place, inviting not just my parents but also my best friend and my sister, creating a comfortable and familiar atmosphere for the introduction.

As my parents walked in, I introduced David. They were already acquainted with my friend and mistakenly assumed David was with her, given I had never mentioned him before. The evening unfolded with a touch of humour and curiosity. David, comfortable and confident, navigated my kitchen with ease, a fact that didn't escape my mother's notice. She shadowed him, intrigued yet puzzled, trying to place him in the familiar context of our family dynamics.

Their exchange was brief but memorable. Mum asked, 'You Italian?' to which David replied, 'No.' Then she probed, 'You speak Italian?' Again, David answered, 'No.' Her final 'oh' carried a mix of resignation and curiosity. Despite the language barrier—my parents spoke very basic English—they managed to get by, but the conversation that evening was minimal.

It wasn't until the baptism day the following week that my parents fully understood that David was not just a friend but my boyfriend. This revelation, set against the backdrop of a family celebration, marked a significant turn in our relationship, officially bringing David into the family fold under the watchful eyes of my parents.

After the baptism, my parents inquired more about David, asking who he was and where he came from. When I revealed that he was a divorcee with two children, my father, for the first time, openly expressed his concerns about my choice. He worried that David wasn't serious and was merely toying with his daughter. Despite his apprehensions, I reassured him, sensing that his protective instincts were stirred by memories of past pains he wished me to avoid. Every time Dad met David, he just grunted at him, making it difficult for David to feel welcomed.

The turning point came when David decided to formally ask for my hand in marriage. We organised a special dinner intended for him to ask for my father's blessing. The evening was filled with playful interruptions; every time David attempted to speak with my father, my siblings and I would distract Dad, enjoying the suspense and watching David sweat. Eventually, David managed to convey his intentions, and from that day forward, my father's attitude towards him changed dramatically. No longer did he just grunt; their relationship began to blossom.

David's ongoing divorce was nothing short of acrimonious; his ex-wife seemed determined to make the process as painful as possible, complicating not just his life but ours together. Each visit from his children was a blend of joy and subsequent challenges. We would spend our weekends exploring new places, ensuring they experienced adventures they'd never had before. I'd often cover the expenses during these trips, as David's financial obligations for maintenance and personal expenses limited his spending ability.

The children would return to their mother elated, yet their moods shifted drastically with each visit, tainted by their mother's disparaging remarks about us. This pattern repeated relentlessly, her hostility manifesting in refusing even to pick up the children if they were anywhere near my house. David would drive substantial distances just to meet her halfway, often returning from these exchanges nearly in tears. Her tactics were those of a bully, making his limited time with his children painfully difficult.

Eventually, the strain began to wear on our relationship. One Sunday night, after a particularly taxing weekend with the kids, I reached my breaking point. I told David that the drama and stress were too much for me at this stage in my life. Opting for solitude over unhappiness, I ended our relationship.

However, after a night of reflection, I reconsidered. My feelings for David and the good moments we shared compelled me to reach out and apologise, suggesting we discuss how to handle the situation moving forward. Our conversation led to a reconciliation, but I knew something had to change. I decided to address the issue directly by writing a letter to his ex-wife, laying out the emotional toll her actions were taking and asserting the need for peace.

Surprisingly, this seemed to shift her perspective. It wasn't until she entered a new relationship with someone who was also navigating the complexities of a blended family that her attitude softened. While we never became friends, her interactions with me became markedly more civil.

In 1997, my professional journey took a significant turn. As my business flourished, I faced a new challenge at home—David moved in with me, occupying what had been my home office. This shift prompted me to relocate my business operations to a small office in Carlton, marking a major transition from a home-based setup to a more formal business environment. This move not only symbolised the expansion of the business but also accommodated our changing personal lives.

David, leaving his position at the Arts Centre, joined the business as an employee. He brought a wealth of knowledge in IT and software development, areas in which I had little expertise. His skills were immediately beneficial, allowing us to enhance our operational capabilities significantly. This integration of advanced technology improved our efficiency and expanded the services we offered, helping to attract a broader range of clients, from local small businesses to large corporations around the globe.

With the business booming, it wasn't long before we outgrew the initial office space. We moved to a larger office and expanded our team to manage the increasing workload and complexity of the projects. This growth was exhilarating, but not without its challenges, particularly in my personal life.

Despite these professional successes, my personal life faced trials, especially with David's children. Their adjustment to the new family dynamics was fraught with difficulties. Their behaviour became a continuous challenge, straining our relationship. These ongoing issues cast a shadow over our forthcoming wedding, stirring doubts and testing my resolve.

To make our living arrangement more comfortable, with five of us now in the house, I transformed the garage into a family room to give the children their own space. However, the relationship with them saw little improvement; their resistance and occasional unruliness were disheartening.

The tension peaked as the wedding neared. My family tried to embrace the children as their own, but the efforts seemed unreciprocated. This difficult situation lingered until the very day of the wedding, leaving me to contemplate my choices deeply.

As I prepared to walk down the aisle, a last-minute wave of doubt nearly halted everything. It was a moment of intense introspection, where I nearly backed out, questioning the path I had chosen after years of independence. The journey to the altar was not just a walk but a profound leap of faith into a new chapter of my life, shaped by both love and the complexities of blending families.

On the 20th of February, 1999, amidst the doubts and the intricate challenges of blending a new family, I walked down the aisle. At 42, marrying at this stage of my life brought a sense of completion and joy not just to me but also to my parents, who had long hoped to see this day. I chose to keep my maiden name upon marrying, firmly believing that one's identity isn't bound by taking another's name. You are who you are; no name change can alter your essence.

For the ceremony, I made a significant choice that both my parents walk me down the garden path. This decision stemmed from my belief that no one should 'give you away'—a notion that felt outdated and misaligned with my values. Instead, having both parents by my side was a symbol of their equal importance in my life and their joint support as I transitioned into this new chapter.

The wedding was held in a beautiful garden, where the natural setting reflected the growth and blossoming of my relationship with David. Despite the earlier uncertainties and the complexity of familial adjustments, the day unfolded beautifully. The garden was alive with the colours of summer, mirroring the warmth and love that surrounded us.

As we exchanged vows, the presence of my parents, walking alongside me, was a poignant reminder of the journey we had all undertaken together—from the days of difficult childhood to the complexities of adult relationships. It was a celebration not just of a union with David but of the enduring bonds with my family, who had seen me through decades of change.

Our wedding day marked not just the start of my married life but also a commitment to blending two families into one harmonious unit. While the road ahead promised its share of challenges, it was also filled with potential for growth, understanding, and deeper connections.

Our marriage journey took a miraculous turn when, at the age of 44, I discovered I was pregnant. The moment it happened, I had an instinctive knowing—a profound connection to the new life beginning inside me. I shared the news with David immediately, who was initially sceptical. However, the real joy and surprise unfolded when the pregnancy test confirmed what I already felt to be true.

Eager to share our unexpected joy, we invited my parents over for dinner to announce the news. Yet, as we revealed our upcoming addition, the response was unexpectedly muted. David, misreading their silence for disapproval, felt a tinge of annoyance. I understood differently; my parents' reaction was rooted in disbelief, not displeasure. Their apparent lack of enthusiasm was simply because they were too accustomed to my penchant for playful pranks over the years.

Life continued, and it wasn't until my pregnancy became visibly obvious that my parents' scepticism turned into overwhelming joy. They finally embraced the reality of the situation, ecstatic about the prospect of a grandchild. Their excitement grew as they anticipated the arrival of a new family member, especially since I had long voiced my intention never to have children.

This period of transformation brought us closer, smoothing over past uncertainties with the shared anticipation of new life. It was a time of preparation and reflection, not just about the kind of parents we would be, but also about how deeply life can surprise and change us, often for the better.

Facing the possibility of complications due to my age, my pregnancy journey required a series of meticulous medical tests to ensure the health of the fetus.

Prior to undergoing these initial tests, David and I engaged in several in-depth discussions regarding the potential outcomes and our course of action should the tests reveal any health issues, such as Down syndrome or spina bifida. I was firm in my decision that, if any serious conditions were detected, we would choose to terminate the pregnancy. This decision was driven not by a lack of love or desire for the child, but by pragmatic considerations of my age and the long-term well-being of the child. Given my stage in life, I was acutely aware of the challenges and responsibilities that would extend far beyond my capacity to provide care in the future. I did not want to burden society, nor could I trust it to adequately care for the child once I was no longer able to. This was a heavy but necessary consideration, guiding our agreement and approach to the pregnancy.

The initial blood test astonishingly reflected the health markers of a 21-year-old, which was a profound relief. The subsequent ultrasound reinforced this positive outcome, indicating that everything was developing normally and healthily. However, the next recommended step was an amniocentesis—a procedure particularly advised for expectant mothers of my age to check for fetal abnormalities, including conditions, like Down syndrome, cystic fibrosis, or spina bifida. Typically performed between the 16th and 20th weeks of pregnancy, this test carries a risk of causing miscarriage, a reality that weighed heavily on my mind.

Given the normal results of the earlier tests, I grappled with the decision. The thought of any procedure potentially endangering the pregnancy was daunting. After much contemplation and discussion with David, I decided to decline the amniocentesis. Trusting the positive outcomes we had already received, I chose to focus on maintaining a healthy pregnancy environment, guided by the reassurance that the initial tests provided. This decision, while difficult, felt right for us, respecting both our hopes and the initial medical feedback we had been fortunate to receive.

My pregnancy was a tumultuous journey, marked by physical discomfort and emotional turbulence from the start. My gynaecologist had recommended reading certain books and attending prenatal classes to prepare for childbirth. Reluctantly, I agreed to read one book and attend one class. However, the book instilled more fear than reassurance. After reading just the first chapter, which filled me with dread about pregnancy and dietary restrictions, I had to stop; the anxiety it induced was overwhelming. When I questioned my doctor about the choice of such unsettling material, she explained that it was standard procedure to recommend these resources.

My apprehension only grew after attending a prenatal class where they showed a prolonged and difficult birth. Witnessing this, I experienced a panic attack, filled with a sudden, intense fear of childbirth—I even momentarily wished to end the pregnancy. Until that class, I had never seen a birth, and the reality shook me deeply.

The physical symptoms during the first trimester only compounded my distress. I was sick constantly, necessitating medication to manage the severe nausea. My diet changed drastically; I couldn't stand the smell of alcohol, except for the occasional beer, and even my beloved coffee became repulsive. Instead, I craved salads, fruits, and vegetables. My iron levels dropped significantly due to my aversion to meat and eggs.

As the pregnancy progressed, the discomfort grew. The final three months were particularly agonising. The weight of my growing child strained my knee so severely that I could not walk without crutches. I felt as though my body was split in two, marked by a visible line from my breast to my navel. My ribs felt like they were fracturing under the pressure, and the constant pain was excruciating, haunting me day and night.

At a pivotal appointment, I broached the topic of childbirth options with my doctor, deliberating between natural birth and a caesarean section. Given my baby's size, I expressed concerns about the feasibility of a natural birth, leaning towards a caesarean for both our well-being. My gynaecologist, visibly relieved by my inclination, concurred emphatically. She reassured me that opting for a caesarean was indeed prudent, prioritising the health and safety of both the baby and myself in our unique situation.

As my due date approached, the discomfort became unbearable, and I pleaded with my gynaecologist to schedule the birth sooner. I had a specific date in mind, the 1st of July. It wasn't just any day; it was the birthday of my favourite singer, John Farnham, making it a perfect dual celebration. However, due to my gynaecologist's schedule—she didn't work on Mondays—my son was born a day later, on Tuesday, the 2nd of July.

Even on the day of the scheduled caesarean, my dedication to my work was undiminished. I spent the morning in my office, tying up loose ends and ensuring everything was in order. This commitment meant I arrived at the hospital half an hour late for my appointment. Despite the rush and the overwhelming emotions, stepping into the hospital marked the culmination of a challenging journey and the beginning of a new, joyous chapter.

When they handed me my newborn, my initial reaction was hesitation—not from lack of love, but due to the blood that covered him. My discomfort with medical sights meant I needed him cleaned before I could embrace him fully. Once cleaned, I held my son, marvelling at his large blue eyes and thick black hair. Weighing 8.8 pounds, his chubby cheeks perfectly complemented his adorable features. No wonder his presence felt so monumental within my small frame; he had, quite literally, split me in two.

While in the hospital, the nurses encouraged me to breastfeed, a choice I was initially open to. However, my baby simply did not take to it; he struggled to latch on. In response, the nurses expressed my milk, but it wasn't sufficient for my voracious little one. By the second day, I firmly requested that they start bottle-feeding him. They prepared a 125 ml bottle of formula, which he eagerly consumed.

The next day, despite continued pressure from the nurses to try breastfeeding again, I stood my ground, choosing formula feeding instead. They reiterated that 'breast milk is best,' but it was clear my son preferred the formula, and I wanted what was best for him. From that point on, we exclusively used formula, and he thrived, growing healthily and contentedly.

He slept through the night for a full 12 hours, allowing both of us some much-needed rest. His satisfaction with the formula meant there was no need for middle-of-the-night feedings; he was content and full, ensuring peaceful nights for us both.

The week of my hospital stay was a blur of business and well-wishers. My VIP room transformed into a hybrid of a gift shop and florist, bustling with visitors and floral scents. However, a week into recovery at home, I began to feel trapped by the confinement of the four walls. The need to return to work gnawed at me—I craved the freedom and normalcy of my routine. After consulting my doctor, I learned I could drive as long as the vehicle was automatic, which, fortuitously, mine was. Thus, David assumed the role of stay-at-home dad, and I returned to work, seeking solace in the familiar whirl of my professional life.

Many women describe pregnancy as a beautiful and joyous time; however, my experience was starkly different. It was the most challenging period of my life. I believe in sharing my truth candidly. Whenever other women ask about my pregnancy, I don't shy away from recounting the struggles I faced. I tell them how it was genuinely the worst time for me, marked by severe discomfort and profound anxiety. This honesty isn't about sowing fear; it's about acknowledging that not every pregnancy experience is idyllic, and that's perfectly valid.

As I navigated the early days of motherhood with a return to the bustling rhythm of my career, I found myself at a crossroads of identity and responsibility. The joy and tumult of bringing a new life into the world juxtaposed with my unyielding commitment to my profession posed challenges that were both exhilarating and daunting. This period of my life was a testament to the strength I had cultivated over the years—balancing the tenderness of motherhood with the assertiveness of a business leader.

Yet, as this chapter closed with me stepping back into the office, a new set of challenges awaited. The upcoming chapter will explore the evolution of my professional life as it intertwines with my role as a new mother, along with the shifting dynamics at home and in the workplace. It was a time of profound personal growth and redefinition, where every day brought both hurdles and triumphs.

Chapter 7

Bridging Worlds: Heritage, Leadership, and Community Resilience

Finding harmony within the chaos was not just a goal but a necessity. This is the story of that intricate dance between motherhood and professional life, between the past and the future. It is about weaving the rich tapestry of my Italian heritage with the practicality of Australian culture, ensuring my son grows up with a deep understanding of both worlds.

After my son was born, I felt a renewed urge to reconnect with my Italian roots. It wasn't just about teaching him about where he came from—it was about immersing him in the rich traditions, the vibrant celebrations, and the warm, communal spirit that defined my upbringing. I wanted to pass on the legacy of Sunday family feasts, where stories flowed as freely as the wine and life lessons were served with every dish. This cultural heritage, steeped in centuries of history and resilience, was a gift I was eager to give my son, alongside the laid-back, egalitarian Australian way of life that his father would introduce.

The juxtaposition of these cultures within our home became a daily exploration. We celebrated Australian holidays with the same enthusiasm as Italian festivals. I taught my son Italian songs and stories, cooking with him as my mother had cooked with me. Our kitchen—a classroom for language, culture, and family bonds.

But my desire to pass on this cultural heritage extended beyond our home. I engaged more actively in the community, participating in cultural events and working with local Italian organisations. This involvement was not just about preserving my identity; it was also a way of creating a bridge between my past and my son's future, ensuring he understood the richness of his heritage.

As he grew, so did his curiosity about his dual heritage. He would ask questions, eager to understand why we celebrated certain festivals or why our food was different from his friends'. Each question was an opportunity to deepen his appreciation for his roots, and with each answer, I found myself reconnecting with my own past, seeing it anew through his eyes.

This chapter of my life, marked by the birth of my son and the subsequent blending of cultures in our home, was a testament to the power of heritage and the beauty of diversity. It was about finding harmony in the chaos of differing traditions and building a family legacy that was uniquely ours. This journey was not just about teaching my son about his heritage; it was about showing him how to live it, breathe it, and ultimately, love it as I did. As we navigate this ongoing journey, the stories of past generations find new life, and the traditions we cherish continue to shape our family's story, echoing through our celebrations, our meals, and our everyday interactions. This is not just the story of one family's cultural fusion; it is a narrative that resonates with anyone who has ever strived to honour their heritage while embracing a new one. It is a reminder of the delicate balance between respecting where we come from and embracing where we are going, all while building a life that respects both.

As my office was located in Lygon Street, Carlton, often referred to as the Little Italy of Melbourne, I joined the Carlton Traders Association. The committee, recognising my creativity and fresh ideas, encouraged me to become more involved. However, based on past experiences where I ended up doing most of the work while others took the credit, I stipulated that I would only join if elected as president. At the Annual General Meeting, I was honoured to be appointed as the president of a precinct I had always cherished.

However, the role came with its own set of challenges, particularly the intricate politics of the area. The precinct was divided between two associations that could not see eye to eye, each representing different segments of local commerce. My task was to merge these two factions into a single entity, as the City of Melbourne would only fund one association in the area. After six months of relentless meetings and negotiations, I succeeded in uniting them under the new name, The Carlton Business Association, a title chosen to encompass all businesses in the area and to avoid favouring one group over the other.

One significant challenge was the membership; the association had only ten paid members, and the council required a minimum of fifty to qualify for funding. Therefore, the fee structure was reframed to include three tiers of membership: individual, small business, and corporate, each with a different price point. This strategy was successful, and within the first year, we had in excess of 100 paid members from various fields of business.

We worked closely not only with the businesses but also with the residents, as they were an integral part of the area. After all, they needed to shop locally, so why not work with them and encourage their support for our council initiatives? I attended the residents' association meetings as much as possible to foster this relationship.

Since 1978, the Lygon Street Festa has become a popular annual event, introducing Australia to the concept of outdoor street festivals and drawing enormous crowds in the hundreds of thousands. However, by the time I took office, the Festa was nearly defunct and had unexpectedly fallen into private hands. These obstacles required diligent navigation of diverse personalities and interests to revive the community spirit and ensure the festival's return to its public roots.

Some of the most significant events I managed to attract to Lygon Street included high-profile activities and community gatherings that not only brought the community together but also highlighted the cultural richness of the area. Among these were the Launch of the Spring Racing Carnival, which brought a flurry of fashion and festivity to the streets, and the Grand Prix Media Launch, which paired local charm with international excitement. Melbourne Fashion Week was another feather in our cap, drawing attention to local designers and boutiques that thrived on the precinct's vibrant scene.

One of the most illustrious events I championed, despite facing considerable opposition and even legal threats from several city councillors, was the grand celebration of Ferrari's 60th Anniversary on March 3, 2007. This monumental occasion drew tens of thousands to Melbourne's Lygon Street, as part of the 2007 Grand Prix Festival. This celebration was not just any event; it was a spectacular prelude to the 2007 Formula 1™ ING Australian Grand Prix, orchestrated as a joint initiative between the Australian Grand Prix Corporation, Ferrari, and the City of Melbourne. Lygon Street was transformed into a vibrant sea of red, capturing the essence and excitement of Ferrari's legacy. This event remains etched in the memories of attendees and continues to be celebrated as a pivotal moment in Melbourne's cultural history, a testament to overcoming adversity and transforming challenge into triumph.

The community also came together for events like the Mother's Day celebrations, which became a hallmark for family gatherings in the area. Additionally, our response to global events was marked by fundraising for the Tsunami relief efforts, showcasing the community's empathy and global consciousness.

Cultural celebrations like La Befana and the La Dolce Italia Festival were particularly close to my heart. They brought Italian traditions to the forefront and celebrated them with the wider Melbourne community. These events not only fostered a deeper understanding and appreciation of Italian culture but also attracted tourists and locals alike, boosting local business and community morale.

I also initiated events aimed at business engagement, such as Business Networking nights and Film Nights, which provided platforms for local entrepreneurs and creatives to collaborate and showcase their talents. The Carnevale on Lygon and the Motor Grand Prix Launch were other standout events that brought dynamism and excitement to the area, drawing crowds in the thousands and significantly enhancing the profile of Lygon Street.

Through these diverse and successful events, I was able to transform Lygon Street into a bustling, vibrant destination, reaffirming its nickname as the Little Italy of Melbourne. Each event not only added to the precinct's allure but also cemented its reputation as a cultural and social hub, drawing visitors from across Melbourne and beyond. In addition to the various cultural and community events, I also worked closely with iconic local institutions like La Mama Theatre and Cinema Nova. These collaborations were instrumental in enriching the cultural landscape of Lygon Street.

La Mama Theatre, a cornerstone of Melbourne's performing arts scene, provided a platform for avant-garde and grassroots theatre. Our partnership involved co-hosting theatrical performances and workshops that drew theatre enthusiasts to Lygon Street, enhancing its reputation as a cultural hub. These events were not just entertainment; they were a celebration of local talent and an expression of our community's creative spirit.

Similarly, my collaboration with Cinema Nova helped integrate film culture deeply into the community activities. We organised Film Nights that featured both mainstream and independent films, turning these events into highly anticipated community gatherings. Cinema Nova, known for its support of independent cinema, was the perfect partner to help promote a diverse cinematic experience, further establishing Lygon Street as a destination for arts and culture enthusiasts.

Through these partnerships, we not only boosted the local economy by attracting more visitors but also strengthened the bonds within the community, fostering a shared sense of identity and pride. Each event, whether a film screening or a theatre production, was a thread in the fabric of our community tapestry, contributing to a vibrant, dynamic precinct that celebrated its cultural richness and diversity.

After 15 years of ongoing disputes between residents and traders with no resolution in sight, I took the initiative to reconcile their differing visions for the piazza. The traders envisioned a large piazza featuring underground parking, while residents preferred a smaller piazza with an expansive park and no parking facilities. Through careful negotiation, we reached a compromise where the piazza would occupy one side of the area, allowing the remaining space to be preserved as a park for communal enjoyment. However, plans for an underground car park were shelved due to financial constraints, making the project more feasible. In 2006, the piazza was officially opened by the Lord Mayor at the time, John So, whose cooperation was invaluable throughout the process. Working with John and his team was a highlight of my career; his dedication to serving the community set a standard that has yet to be matched by subsequent city leaders.

My seven-year tenure as the president and representative of the Lygon Street Precinct was a profoundly rewarding period of my professional life. During this time, I devoted myself entirely to the precinct's events and marketing, choosing to offer my services without charge. My intention was clear: to ensure that all available funding could be directed towards revitalising the precinct to its former glory.

Being on call 24/7 for the precinct, my life was almost entirely consumed by this role. My husband was understandably unhappy with the relentless demands on my time, which often came at the expense of our personal life. Despite these challenges, I was pivotal in ensuring that the 60th-anniversary celebrations of Ferrari proceeded despite opposition. Facing councillors who wanted the event cancelled, I stood firm, even under the threat of legal action. This was not unfamiliar territory for me; my life has been a series of battles for what I believed in, and I have never been one to be intimidated by opposition, particularly from men.

After seven fruitful years as president of the Lygon Street Precinct, I was approached to run for a local council. Initially, I hesitated; my political views are staunch, and I've often found the bureaucratic red tape stifling, hindering progress more than facilitating it. However, after thoughtful discussions with my husband and considerable reflection on my own, I decided to step into the political arena. I believed that my deep involvement in community events and my unwavering commitment could genuinely contribute to broader, positive changes across the city.

In 2008, I launched my council campaign, fuelled by a vision to leverage my on-ground experiences and the successes I had spearheaded in the Lygon Street Precinct. This move was a natural extension of my lifelong dedication to public service and community advocacy, driven by the same passion that had defined my tenure with the traders' association. Unfortunately, being third on the ticket meant my chances were slim, and I did not secure a seat. Despite this, the campaign journey reinforced my commitment to effecting change and serving the community in whatever capacities I could.

This decision marked the end of an era and the beginning of another as I scaled back my extensive community involvement to focus more on my growing family. However, I continued my engagement with the community by continuing as the marketing and communication officer for the Police Community Consultative Committee. Simultaneously, my passion for event management led me to start a new business specialising in event management, which kept me active in Lygon Street's vibrant scene until 2011.

After I stepped down, finding a successor for my role as president of the Lygon Street Precinct proved challenging. Initially, no one was eager to take on the responsibilities. However, after considerable persuasion, we managed to find someone who accepted the position on the condition that I remained involved, especially in managing events. This arrangement aligned perfectly with my new business focus.

I made it clear that the association should not operate like a family business. I encouraged the new president to actively engage with other traders and maintain the open, inclusive atmosphere I had nurtured. My approach had always been to 'spread the love,' positioning myself as a partner rather than a competitor, which had earned me the trust and appreciation of the traders.

Unfortunately, the new president did not take my advice to heart. The association soon turned inward under his leadership, becoming a closed circle dominated by his family. This shift led to a lack of transparency, and soon, many in the precinct felt out of the loop, unaware of the association's activities and decisions. This lack of openness marked a significant departure from the inclusivity that had characterised my tenure.

Worse still, the new president actively worked against the efforts to revive the local festival. He went behind my back, misleading the council by claiming that the traders opposed the event. This deception wasted considerable time, as I had to gather petitions and demonstrate genuine community support for the festival—a frustrating setback that underscored the challenges of leadership transitions in community organisations.

During this period, one of the traders on Lygon Street came up with an ambitious idea: to attempt to break the Guinness World Record for the longest pizza. Enthusiastic about the concept, I agreed to handle the administrative aspects—such as registration, promotion, and securing sponsorship. The City of Melbourne provided funding, which significantly boosted our promotional efforts.

However, as the event drew closer, my anxiety escalated. Despite repeated attempts to check in, the trader tasked with crafting the pizza was perpetually too busy to update me. This mounting concern reminded me of a fortunate encounter a few months prior at an event hosted by the Italian Chamber of Commerce in Melbourne and the Italian Consul General of Melbourne and Tasmania. There, I met a chef whose vision for Italian cultural events echoed my own aspirations.

When I shared the idea of attempting the longest pizza record, his enthusiasm was palpable. He immediately suggested a meeting to discuss how he could help, infusing the project with renewed optimism and a shared excitement for showcasing Italian culture. As the day of the meeting dawned, I prepared my office to welcome the chef whose shared enthusiasm for the longest pizza record could catapult Lygon Street back into the cultural spotlight. The air buzzed with potential as I arranged the venue, envisioning our collaboration as the beginning of something grand, a celebration of Italian heritage that Melbourne would remember for years.

However, as I greeted him at the door of my office, I could not have predicted that this encounter would lead to the most significant regret of my life. What began with shared laughs and dreams of grandeur, surrounded by the familiar confines of my workspace, would soon spiral into an unforeseen series of challenges and setbacks. This meeting, marked by a handshake beneath the framed photos of past successful events, was poised to be a turning point, not just for our project but for my entire professional journey.

This was the precipice of my downfall—the moment before the plunge. What transpired in the aftermath of this meeting would challenge my resilience and shape the future in ways I had never imagined. Turn the page to Chapter 8, where the true test of my career and character begins.

Chapter 8

A Promising Beginning

The office door closed with a soft click, leaving a lingering sense of new possibilities in the air. The meeting with the chef had ended on a note of palpable excitement, his enthusiasm infecting every corner of the room. As I sat back in my chair, the early shadows of doubt were quickly overshadowed by the promising plans we had laid out together.

He had come prepared, not just with innovative ideas but with a concrete plan that seemed almost too good to be true. The quote he presented was substantial, yet he assured me it wouldn't touch the event's budget. 'Don't worry about the costs,' he had said with a confident smile. 'I have sponsors lined up who are just waiting for my signal. They're as excited about this as we are, and they're ready to cover everything.'

The idea of hosting the world's longest pizza record without a financial strain was exhilarating. It meant that not only could we bring a spectacular event to life, but it would also be financially feasible, a rare combination in the world of large-scale public events. His assurance that sponsors were already onboard and eager to participate added an extra layer of security to the project.

Flushed with a mix of relief and excitement, I began to envision the streets of Lygon lined with enthusiastic crowds, the air filled with the aroma of fresh pizza, and the buzz of a community coming together for a record-setting day. It seemed like everything was aligning perfectly, setting the stage for an event that would go down in history.

With a newfound energy, I started to map out the next steps, ready to dive into the logistics and promotional strategies. The chef's promise of sponsorship was a cornerstone of our plans, a crucial element that would allow us to aim for heights we hadn't thought possible.

Turn the page to follow the journey of turning this grand vision into reality, a path filled with excitement, challenges, and the thrill of pushing boundaries in ways I had never imagined.

As plans for the longest pizza world record unfolded, the initial excitement mingled with mounting challenges. The chef, while seemingly enthusiastic, was difficult to reach by phone, and the much-anticipated sponsorships faltered; companies expressed interest but cited budget timing issues, offering services at cost rather than financial support. Despite these setbacks, the event gained significant media attention, compelling us to press forward.

The event kicked off on a Saturday night with a short film competition judged by an Emmy Award-winning director from Italy, setting a prestigious tone. However, the weather had other plans; what began as a light drizzle escalated into a downpour, forcing us to cancel the film night prematurely.

The preparation for the pizza began under less-than-ideal conditions. Of the 300 volunteers the chef claimed had registered, only a few showed up, their absence blamed on the relentless rain. Trusting the chef's explanations, I pushed on, but anxiety loomed as the dough was mixed and cooking commenced in the early hours.

The goal was clear: stretch the pizza to 1.2 kilometres to clinch the world record. As midday approached, with the festival scheduled to start, the rain persisted, prompting the council to pressure me for a cancellation. Requesting a mere 30 minutes to make a final decision, fortune finally favoured us—the rain ceased right on cue. With a collective sigh of relief, the festival began, albeit under a cloud of stress and wet weather challenges, marking a day of endurance and celebration.

The event unfolded with incredible success, drawing an impressive crowd of over 87,000 attendees, as estimated by the police. The vibrant atmosphere filled Lygon Street, and local traders thrived amid the bustling crowd. However, despite the excitement and strong turnout, we did not achieve the world record due to a significant tear in the pizza at the 600-metre mark. Consequently, we had to call off the record attempt.

Nonetheless, the media coverage was extraordinary, catapulting the event into international headlines. My phone was buzzing with calls from all corners of the globe, and notably, the event made waves in the Asian media markets of Japan and China. The widespread attention was more than I could have hoped for, and despite the setback with the record, the event was a resounding success in many other ways.

Buoyed by the event's success, the chef expressed his enthusiasm about our collaboration and proposed that we organise it again, asking me to become a partner. While I was open to working together again, I chose to involve him in a different capacity, not as a partner in my primary event management business but within another dormant company I planned to activate. This arrangement ensured that the new venture had no existing assets or liabilities, keeping the slate clean for what we might build together.

To formalise our collaboration, I engaged my lawyer to draft a partnership agreement. The process involved numerous revisions, with the document going back and forth between the chef and my lawyer to ensure every detail was meticulously outlined, preventing any potential disputes in the future. This careful legal groundwork was crucial to setting a firm foundation for our new joint venture.

Plans for expanding the festival were taking shape as we contemplated transforming it into an Italian exhibition, tapping into the potential for business opportunities between Italian companies and Australian markets. The chef, who claimed to come from a highly influential and affluent family in Italy, shared that his father's approval was essential for any significant business move within Italy. His assertiveness and detailed accounts of his family's prominence were compelling. He spoke with such authority and charisma about his connections and the potential to bring numerous Italian companies to Australia that I was swept up by his vision. Believing in the authenticity and potential of his connections, I agreed to proceed with the plans, excited by the prospect of creating a more expansive cultural and business exchange.

The division of responsibilities was clear: The chef took charge of securing Italian company participation, managing sponsorship, and overseeing the food segments, particularly the pizza showcase, while I focused on venue coordination, fashion, and entertainment, areas where I had established expertise. He also arranged meetings with various marketing and PR firms, eventually settling on one that we placed on a monthly retainer after several discussions to ensure they aligned with our vision for the event.

For ticketing, we opted for a company recommended by the chef, someone within his network. Initially, they appeared competent and well-organised, which reassured me about their involvement.

An intriguing arrangement emerged regarding sponsorships. The chef explained that invoicing would need to be handled through his own company, citing established relationships with potential sponsors that insisted on this method due to existing ties with his business. He assured me that once payments were made, he would promptly transfer the funds to our event account.

This setup, while unusual, didn't immediately raise alarms due to the chef's persuasive assurance and the apparent legitimacy of his connections. Trusting his expertise and the relationships he claimed to have, I focused on my sectors of the project, hopeful that our collaborative efforts would lead to a successful and impactful event.

As the event drew nearer, the financial pressures intensified. The chef transferred a single payment of $10,000 to the business account, but it was a mere drop in the ocean compared to the growing pile of invoices. His reassurances that the funds from ticket sales and sponsors would soon cover all expenses provided some comfort, yet the reality of the financial shortfall was becoming starkly evident.

We were projecting between 15,000 to 20,000 attendees over the three-day festival, which, under normal circumstances, should have generated enough revenue to handle the costs. However, the anticipated sponsor contributions from Italy, crucial for balancing the books, remained conspicuously absent.

In a bid to keep the event on track, I found myself increasingly relying on personal resources. I diverted funds from my other business operations and maxed out my credit cards to cover immediate expenses, including the travel and accommodation costs for several key Italian guests—a pastry chef, a culinary chef, and a renowned hairdresser. Each expense was a gamble on the success of the event, a bet made more daunting as my credit card statements grew and for the first time, I was unable to pay off the balances in full.

The trickle of funds from the ticketing company was insufficient, and with each passing day, my financial anxiety deepened. The chef's continued promises of imminent funding began to ring hollow, leaving me to juggle creditors and dwindling resources, all while striving to maintain the quality and integrity of the event I had envisioned.

The stress of the event planning took a significant toll on both my professional and personal life. As the event approached, the chef's absences became more frequent. He was seldom available during the day and often unresponsive, and his explanations centred on endless meetings. It seemed he was orchestrating operations on a national scale, yet the tangible results of these meetings were nowhere to be seen.

His expectation for the team to work nocturnally only added to the strain. Night after night, we toiled, pushing through to the early hours, while he remained elusive about his daytime activities. This erratic schedule began to put a severe strain on my relationship with my husband, who saw the toll it was taking on my health and questioned the productivity of such gruelling hours.

Despite my mounting concerns and my husband's warnings, I defended the chef's commitment to the project, clinging to the hope that his efforts during the day would eventually pay off. However, as we edged closer to the event, the financial uncertainties could no longer be ignored. When I pressed the chef for assurances about the funding, his stark admission that he had no money left me reeling. I was angry and his only answer to that was to cancel the event. I couldn't believe that after spending all this money, he wanted me to cancel the event, which meant that I would have to further find funds to refund the money from the tickets, which we had already used some of. This revelation threatened not just the event's viability but also the financial stability I had worked so hard to maintain.

My office had become overrun with the chef's personnel, each billing our company for their involvement. Among them was an individual who seemed unconditionally devoted to the chef—his loyalty was so pronounced that it bordered on adulation. His reverence was unsettling, especially given the chef's dismissive and harsh treatment of his own girlfriend, who, despite her evident infatuation, was subjected to constant verbal abuse.

The chef's behaviour towards her was not just rude; it was demeaning and cruel. Witnessing this in my own workplace, where respect should have been paramount, became increasingly unbearable. One evening, pushed to my limit by his degrading tirades, I confronted him. I asserted that any such behaviour in my office was unequivocally my concern. I demanded they take their personal disputes outside.

Reluctantly, they moved their argument into the street, continuing the confrontation under the dim streetlights. The scene was not just a personal embarrassment for them but a professional one for me, marking a stark, public display of the dysfunction that had seeped into my professional space. This incident underscored the volatile and uncomfortable atmosphere the chef had cultivated around him, one that clashed profoundly with the values I upheld in my business and personal life.

We had marketed the event as a true Italian affair, showcasing the finest aspects of Italian culture with an array of food, wine, and fashion imported directly from Italy. However, the reality soon diverged from these initial promises. The chef's solution to the unexpectedly sparse exhibitor turnout was to utilise his importing business to supply the event. Unfortunately, the booths were not only undermanned but also staffed by individuals who lacked crucial knowledge about the products they were selling.

Amidst this disarray, a significant crisis erupted with an Italian/Iranian architect and artist, reputed to be a prince, who had been invited to showcase his artwork. The chef had promised him support in finding exhibition space, a commitment that was not met upon his arrival. When the artist and his partner saw the state of the event, their frustration boiled over. They vehemently expressed their dismay and threatened to leave the event, which could have severely damaged its reputation due to the extensive marketing that had highlighted his participation.

Faced with the potential disaster of losing a prominently featured artist, we sought assistance from the Italian Consul General, who intervened effectively. With his involvement, we organised a month-long exhibition for the artist at the Italian Cultural Institute. This resolution, while stabilising, underscored the extent of mismanagement and broken promises that had plagued the event's organisation. It was a stark reminder of the challenges I faced, adding to the overwhelming burden I was already carrying.

The morning of the event brought an unexpected and unsettling update. The ticketing company informed me that the chef and they had jointly decided against counting the number of attendees, deeming it unnecessary. This decision was a shock to me, leaving me feeling helpless as the event unfolded.

Despite the lower-than-expected turnout, my estimation based on years of event management experience was that we had welcomed between 8,000 to 10,000 attendees. When I requested the official numbers from the ticketing company, they startlingly reported only about 2,000 attendees. This figure did not align with the activity I had witnessed over the three days.

Dutifully, I reported this number in my acquittal report to the venue. However, this led to a prompt call from the venue's manager, who had been present throughout the event. He challenged the figure, suggesting that it seemed more likely we had missed adding a 'one' before the 'two,' indicating we should have reported around 12,000 attendees. I clarified that the figure I reported was directly from the ticketing company. The venue manager expressed disbelief, recalling a much busier event, aligning with my initial estimate of 8,000 to 10,000 attendees.

He questioned whether the ticketing company had been clicking counts as attendees entered, to which I relayed the earlier decision to forego counting. The venue manager found this approach highly irregular and suggested that something wasn't adding up with the ticketing company's operations. This discrepancy not only affected the financial outcomes but also cast doubt on the reliability and integrity of the processes supposedly managed by the chef and the ticketing company.

Upon confronting both the chef and the ticketing company about the discrepancies in attendee numbers, they staunchly defended their reported figure of 2,000, insisting that both the venue and I were mistaken. This denial was baffling and further highlighted the gravity of my oversight in trusting them without stricter oversight.

The situation escalated when I discovered that no sponsorship funds had been received. To my dismay, I also received an unexpected invoice from the chef's importing company. He brazenly claimed that he had redirected the sponsorship funds to cover this invoice, a move made without my consent. This act of misappropriation was startling and left me feeling utterly deceived.

My distress grew during a subsequent meeting with our PR and marketing firm. It was revealed that the chef had manipulated their services to primarily benefit his own business, further exploiting the resources of my company. Shocked by this revelation, I immediately ceased all payments to the PR firm and directed them to seek compensation from the chef's company directly.

Feeling utterly betrayed and manipulated, I sought legal counsel. During a meeting arranged by my lawyer with the chef, it became painfully clear to both my lawyer and me that the chef was nothing more than a con artist. My lawyer's immediate recognition of the chef's deceptive nature only deepened my regret for having ever involved myself with him. This meeting was not just a confrontation but a stark unveiling of the deceit I had been subjected to, marking a profound moment of realisation about the extent of the exploitation I had endured.

Adding insult to injury, the chef brazenly boasted within the Italian community about making a substantial profit from the event. When I countered these claims, sharing the stark financial losses I had incurred, my words fell on sceptical ears, leaving me further isolated and discredited. This discrepancy between our accounts made me painfully aware that perhaps the chef had indeed profited immensely—at my own expense.

The situation took another turn when one of the sponsors requested a meeting to discuss their return on investment, which they felt was insufficient. The chef had previously assured me that the sponsors had modest expectations, merely seeking visibility for their logos on our printed materials. However, armed with data during the meeting, I was able to demonstrate that contrary to their claims, they had received an ROI that exceeded twenty times their initial investment. This revelation silenced their complaints, and I heard nothing further from them after this vindicating encounter. This small victory was a rare moment of validation amidst the turmoil, yet it did little to mitigate the overall devastation wrought by the chef's deceit.

My lawyer advised that while I could likely win a legal battle against the chef, I would also face certain losses due to the significant legal fees involved. He suspected that the chef didn't have substantial assets, which meant even a legal victory would result in financial loss. Following this counsel, I decided against pursuing the matter in court, choosing instead to close this painful chapter and focus on mitigating the losses I had already suffered.

The weight of my situation was overwhelming. Ashamed and financially devastated, I found myself isolated, too proud to confess the true depth of my crisis. To my husband, I maintained a facade that my business was flourishing; he believed everything was well because I always assured him of our success. Internally, I was crumbling, enveloped in loneliness with nowhere to turn. Despite exhausting every financial avenue available— tapping into my other company's resources and maxing out my credit cards— I was still drowning in a staggering debt of over $400,000. Thoughts of ending my suffering surfaced repeatedly, but the thought of my young son growing up without his mother held me back. I knew I had to persevere, if not for myself, then for him.

It was during this bleak period that I began stealing from a long-standing bookkeeping client who had trusted me implicitly for over 20 years. Initially, my theft was a desperate bid to manage the mounting debts. However, it only drove me deeper into depression, fuelling my compulsion to gamble. Although I managed to pay off most of the debts with the stolen money, my theft continued as I struggled to support my gambling habit. Amid this turmoil, I made a decision that torments me to this day—I embezzled a substantial sum from a client who had become more like family than a friend. He had entrusted me with his life, and by betraying him, I didn't just steal his money; I irrevocably broke his trust. The guilt and shame from this betrayal were crushing, yet my addiction had taken control, sending my life into a downward spiral.

Outwardly, my image remained untarnished. To the public, I was the epitome of a successful, carefree businesswoman. But behind this mask, the only respite I found was in front of the glowing screens of slot machines. There, in the dim lights of the casino, I could drop my facade and momentarily escape the oppressive weight of my dual life.

Devastated and determined to uncover the truth about the con man, I travelled to Italy to delve into his background. Upon arriving in his hometown, the revelations were startling. He had never studied hospitality nor completed high school, contrary to the illustrious image he portrayed.

His life consisted of odd jobs, a far cry from the wealthy entrepreneur he claimed to be. His father was a diligent factory worker at FIAT, his mother a housewife, and his sister worked part-time in a pharmacy to support her family.

The local businesses were equally baffled; they still had goods prepared and ready to ship to Australia, waiting for instructions that never came. My journey unveiled the stark reality: The only reason he was in Australia was due to a young Italian woman who fell in love with him during a vacation. They married, and he took over running their family restaurant in Melbourne, which he subsequently ran into the ground. The financial strain was so severe that they nearly lost their home; the stress contributed to the father's suffering a heart attack and the mother being diagnosed with cancer. Their daughter bore the emotional scars of his verbal and emotional abuse, requiring extensive counselling before she could find peace and trust someone new.

This voyage to Italy not only exposed the lies but also the profound impact of his deceit on innocent lives.

Yet, despite everything, he continued his deceptive practices. It's deeply frustrating that I couldn't publicly name him, for fear of legal repercussions, which meant conning more unsuspecting individuals who would fall victim to his schemes. The awareness that his cycle of deceit remained unbroken added a layer of helplessness to my own recovery journey.

Upon returning to Australia, I learned that his girlfriend had finally left him. We met up, and I shared what I had discovered about him in Italy. She also confided to me that she had suspected his infidelity for some time. She had installed a tracker on his phone, as he was not tech-savvy, and tracked him to numerous hotels. By the time she arrived at these locations, he had already departed. This explained why my calls often went unanswered, not due to business meetings, as he claimed, but because of his escapades. She revealed more about his character, describing him as a mercenary, eagerly waiting for her grandmother's demise to inherit her wealth. This added another layer to the deception, showing his disregard not just for business ethics but also for personal relationships, too.

The revelations from his former girlfriend painted a starkly different picture of the man I once trusted. His manipulations extended beyond the business realm, deeply entangling personal lives. As I pieced together the reality of his deceit, I felt a mixture of relief and revulsion—relief that others had seen through his facade, and revulsion at the extent of his betrayal.

This chapter of my life closed with a heavy heart, laden with lessons about trust and the masks people wear. But with every ending comes a new beginning. As I turned the page, I was determined to rebuild, not just my finances, but my faith in humanity. The next chapter would be one of healing and rediscovery, a journey back to the core values that had guided me before this storm—integrity, resilience, and the relentless pursuit of truth.

Chapter 9

In the aftermath of betrayal and addiction

After betraying and stealing from a dear client to pay off debts, I found myself spiralling into a new obsession: gambling. Though the initial debts were settled, I continued stealing, feeding this insidious addiction to pokie machines. I was captivated by their hypnotic allure—the bright, flashing lights, the intoxicating clinking sounds, and the trance-like state they induced. For those fleeting moments in front of the machines, I could escape the crushing weight of my double life. It was the only place where I could drop the façade of being a successful, happy-go-lucky businesswoman and sit alone with my fractured, broken self.

The casinos knew exactly how to exploit this weakness. They reeled me in with their endless junkets, offering free accommodations, luxurious dinners at high-end restaurants, exclusive invitations to events, and every imaginable luxury to keep me hooked. The more they gave, the more I gambled. It was a vicious cycle that I couldn't break free from, even as the losses piled higher and higher.

I told myself that if I won big, I could make amends and repay my client. But looking back, I see that for the delusion it was. How could I have ever repaid him, even if I had won? The machines didn't pay out—not in the way I needed them to. They only took and took, leaving me with a mountain of losses that I could never climb out of.

On the outside, I maintained the image of a successful businesswoman. I wore a smile that belied the chaos inside. I acted the part, pretending I had everything under control. But inside, I was falling apart. My debts were mounting, my desperation was deepening, and I was consumed by a cycle of fleeting hope followed by crushing despair. Gambling was my escape, my addiction, and my torment. Deep down, I knew I was destroying myself and those who cared for me. But denial had trapped me in a vicious loop, convincing me I could stop anytime I wanted—if only I had the willpower.

During this dark period, my friendship with the Prince became one of the few bright spots in my life—or so I thought. We shared our frustrations and disappointments, bonding over our mutual disdain for a certain chef who had caused us both grief. Over time, he became like family to me. I loved him as if he were my brother, and he told me I was the sister he never had. That sense of connection and trust was comforting at a time when I felt so alone.

We stayed in constant contact, exchanging messages and calls, and meeting whenever I visited Italy. The Prince was full of grand promises—collaborative ventures that seemed full of potential. I wanted to believe that working with him could help me escape the mess I had created and rebuild my life.

Since I travelled to Italy several times a year, he suggested I rent an apartment instead of staying in hotels, explaining that it would be more cost-effective. It seemed like a sensible idea, so I let him handle the arrangements. I reimbursed him for the costs without ever asking for receipts. After all, he was a Prince—why would I question his honesty? He didn't need money, or so I thought.

But this arrangement led to uncomfortable situations. On one occasion, he asked to use the apartment to meet someone he had connected with and requested that I keep it a secret from his partner. It made me uneasy, but I allowed it, telling myself it wasn't my place to judge. Still, these moments left me questioning the dynamics of our friendship.

The Prince had promised to help me find Italian companies to participate in the second edition of a Chinese exhibition I was working on. This event was deeply important to me—it represented a bridge between cultures and an opportunity to create meaningful connections between Italian businesses and Chinese markets. It wasn't just about the event itself; it was about fostering trust, building relationships, and showcasing the best of Italy to the world.

The Prince insisted he needed salespeople to explore different regions in Italy to recruit companies, claiming he couldn't manage it all on his own. He explained it would cost €6,000 per month for six salespeople—a staggering amount of money. Despite the enormity of the cost, I felt I had no choice if I wanted the project to succeed. I trusted him and believed in his vision.

But as months flew by and no companies were signing up, he justified the lack of signings with a series of excuses, painting a bleak picture of the Italian economy and the struggles many companies were facing. According to him, these businesses weren't particularly interested in China but showed great enthusiasm for opportunities in Australia. He convinced me that the allure of Australia would be the key to bringing these companies on board, and so the idea of the Australian exhibition was born—a venture I believed could bridge cultures and create lasting opportunities.

Due to the lack of interest from the Italian companies, according to the Prince, I had no choice but to cancel the Chinese exhibition project. The decision left me bitterly disappointed, especially since the first edition had been so well received by the Chinese. I had even won the award for the best country pavilion—a recognition that filled me with pride and validated the hard work I had poured into it. For that event, I built a massive replica of the Colosseum, transforming it into a stunning Italian piazza with the iconic Trevi Fountain at its heart. The Colosseum itself encircled the space, with its little nooks cleverly designed as exhibitors' booths.

Promoting Italian culture in China had been more than a professional endeavour; it was a passion, a labour of love. This project wasn't just another business venture—it was deeply personal. I had poured so much into it—not only financially but emotionally. I invested every ounce of my energy into making it a success, convinced it could open doors for both Italian businesses and myself. Letting it go felt like a profound loss, a painful reminder of what could have been.

Eventually, the harsh truth became impossible to ignore. The promises I had clung to were hollow, and the Australian/Italian project was crumbling before my eyes. I felt powerless to stop it. Cancelling the entire initiative was one of the hardest decisions I've ever had to make, yet it was just the beginning of many difficult choices that would test me in the journey ahead. It felt like a deeply personal failure—not only to myself but also to everyone who had placed their trust in me and believed in the vision I had worked so tirelessly to bring to life.

My Chinese client, a person I deeply respected, had been unwaveringly supportive throughout the planning process. He had trusted my word, my reputation, and my ability to deliver Italian companies to the exhibition. I vividly remember a moment when he spoke directly to the Prince. After their conversation, he turned to me and asked pointedly, 'Can you trust this person?' Without hesitation, I replied, 'I trust the Prince with my life!' That memory now felt like a painful betrayal of my own judgment.

Having to tell my client that I couldn't follow through was absolutely devastating. The shame and guilt felt crushing. As I listened to his voice on the other end of the call, I could hear the palpable disappointment, and it broke me. This wasn't just the failure of a project—it felt like a failure of character, and the weight of that realisation was almost unbearable.

I wanted so desperately to explain that this failure wasn't entirely my fault—that I had been misled, manipulated, and let down by people I had trusted deeply. But I couldn't. I had always taken personal responsibility for my actions, and admitting otherwise felt like an excuse I wasn't willing to make. In the end, none of that mattered. A promise had been broken, and I was the one left to shoulder the crushing weight of that shattered trust.

The fallout wasn't just professional; it was profoundly personal. I replayed every decision I had made, every moment I had placed my faith in the Prince, wondering where I had gone wrong. Yet, he had been so convincing. I blamed myself for not seeing the warning signs earlier, for failing to ask the right questions, and for putting so much trust in someone who hadn't earned it. The disappointment hung over me like a heavy fog, suffocating and inescapable.

This failure left a scar, one that took a long time to heal. It was a painful reminder of the cost of misplaced trust and the importance of following through on commitments. But it also taught me a valuable lesson about resilience and the need to stay true to my own values, even in the face of adversity.

After the disaster with the Chef as my business partner, I went quiet for a few years until the first edition of the Chinese exhibition reignited my drive. Although the second edition failed to secure Italian companies for China, I remained determined to revive my business. In an effort to breathe new life into my brand, I decided to rebrand my company with an iconic Italian figure.

The Prince and I brainstormed ideas, and I kept coming back to one name: Sophia Loren. At first, the Prince dismissed her as irrelevant, but his friends eventually persuaded him otherwise. He told me he had a contact who knew her manager and could make the arrangements—for a fee of €10,000. Desperate for a breakthrough and captivated by the opportunity, I agreed.

The Prince informed me that Sophia's management had agreed to the terms, including the appearance fee and all travel arrangements. Everything seemed to be falling into place. However, I never spoke to Sophia or her management directly—not once until they arrived in Australia. The Prince handled all communication, insisting that they preferred dealing exclusively through him.

Sophia's visit was more than a prestigious event; it was a lifeline for my business, an opportunity to rebrand after the financial disaster with the con-man chef. It felt like a second chance to prove myself and restore my credibility in the industry.

During this time, the Prince proposed an ambitious idea: organising a grand exhibition in Australia—a trade show featuring Italian companies. The concept was bold and aligned perfectly with my vision of showcasing Italy's best in Australia. Together, we began planning a gala with Sophia Loren for April 2015 and a trade exhibition for October of the same year. The Prince confidently took the lead in coordinating meetings with regional business chambers, promising their full support and active participation.

One particular meeting with an Italian chamber left me ecstatic. They agreed to pay my company €1,500 for each participating company that registered interest and an additional €3,000 for every company that travelled to Australia. It felt like a dream come true—a confirmation that we were on the right path. Fuelled by this optimism, I immediately booked the Melbourne Showgrounds for the exhibition. For the first time in a long while, I felt a glimmer of hope that this could be the turning point I desperately needed.

Everything appeared to be falling into place until the Prince delivered a shocking and unexpected revelation. After our promising meeting with the chamber, he informed me that €600 from each company's original registration fee would need to be paid back in cash to a contact at the chamber, along with €1,500 from the marketing money. He insisted these payments had to be made in cash, with no trace.

I was appalled. The blatant corruption was something I had never encountered, and it went against everything I believed in. Yet, I felt trapped.

Refusing these demands could jeopardise the entire event, undoing all the work and resources I had invested. Reluctantly, I convinced myself that this was a necessary evil to ensure the project's success.

The Prince also introduced me to a female Italian lawyer, who shared our enthusiasm for the exhibition. During my visit to Italy, she introduced us to various industries that were equally keen to participate. Her connections seemed promising, and I felt reassured when she announced an exciting development: she had secured an opportunity for the La Dolce Italia event to be included in the prestigious Milan Expo. This, she said, would provide a double benefit for the participating companies—they could showcase their products in Melbourne and gain additional exposure at the Milan Expo. The Lawyer repeatedly assured me that this wouldn't cost my company a cent, as all expenses were covered by committed sponsors. Her confidence was infectious, and I allowed myself to believe that this event could bridge cultures while creating significant opportunities for Italian businesses.

The La Dolce Italia Expo was envisioned as much more than just a trade show. It was a celebration of Italian culture—its food, fashion, music, and art—designed to create a lasting connection between Italy and Australia. Presented to me as a self-funded, risk-free venture with all sponsorships secured, the event seemed like the perfect plan to bring Italian businesses to the international stage.

However, as the planning progressed, cracks in their promises began to surface. Documents and emails started arriving, outlining commitments I supposedly had to fulfil—commitments I had never agreed to. One document proposed a staggering €270,000 fee for participation in the Milan Expo, a cost that had never been discussed. Then, seemingly out of nowhere, I was informed of a requirement to purchase 10,000 bottles of wine from The Lawyer's husband's winery. These weren't minor requests; they were massive financial obligations that appeared without warning. Each new email brought unexpected twists—additional costs, conditions, and responsibilities that I had neither anticipated nor consented to.

What made it worse was the realisation that the Milan Expo was not just a supplementary component—it was baked into the core of the original plan. I had been led to believe that Milan was meant to complement Melbourne, enhancing the overall experience for participating businesses. Instead, it became clear that Milan had overshadowed Melbourne entirely, relegating it to an afterthought. Many of the Italian companies being enticed to attend the Milan Expo had little intention of coming to Melbourne, despite having paid registration fees for both events. The 'double bonus' they had been promised turned out to be nothing more than a mirage.

The breaking point came when I realised the full extent of these commitments. What had started as a dream of cultural celebration was quickly spiralling into a financial nightmare. Costs for exhibition spaces, artist hires, and promotional activities—all of which were supposed to be covered—were now being thrust onto my shoulders. The partnership I had envisioned had devolved into a crushing burden.

I vividly remember opening an email that stated my company was responsible for setting up a major exhibition space for 180 companies at the Milan Expo—a commitment I had never agreed to and had no way of fulfilling. The realisation that I had been misled and manoeuvred into this position hit me like a punch to the gut. I felt betrayed and foolish for having trusted so blindly once again.

When I raised my concerns with the Prince and emailed both him and The Lawyer to clarify that this was not the agreement, The Lawyer reportedly flew into a rage. According to the Prince, she began threatening to sue me, despite his attempts to calm her down. Finally, I told him to pass on a simple message: 'Tell her to sue me if she wishes.' I was done with the manipulation and coercion.

I made it crystal clear to the Prince that I would neither pay a quarter of a million euros for the Milan Expo nor promote their wine. Saying those words was terrifying—my heart raced, and my hands trembled—but I knew I had to stand my ground. This led to a heated argument between the Prince and The Lawyer. Voices were raised, accusations were hurled, and the tension was suffocating. I felt a strange mix of fear and empowerment, but I refused to back down.

Eventually, the Prince begrudgingly accepted my decision, though his frustration was palpable. For a fleeting moment, I felt triumphant, but that feeling quickly gave way to unease. The promised sponsorships from Italy never materialised, and each broken promise weighed heavily on me. With every passing day, the pressure mounted, and my frustration deepened.

In the end, I had no choice but to cancel the exhibition and continue working with the Prince on the gala with Sophia Loren. It was a devastating blow— not just to me, but to everyone involved. I knew the decision would disappoint many, but there was no other viable path forward. Determined to salvage some part of the project and protect my credibility, I poured my energy into ensuring the success of the gala with Sophia Loren, hoping it could still be a shining moment amid the chaos.

One of my greatest passions in life has always been raising money for charities. For this gala, I partnered with the Alannah & Madeline Foundation, whose mission is to protect children from violence—a cause deeply personal to me, having come from a violent home. This connection made the foundation's work especially meaningful, and it resonated deeply with Sophia as well. She graciously agreed to participate in media interviews, promoting both the gala and the charity. Her support added a powerful touch, amplifying the event's purpose and highlighting the importance of this vital cause.

A few months prior to the gala, I received a phone call from the Prince. He told me that Sophia's manager had contacted him, demanding an additional €50,000 for her appearance—and it had to be paid in cash. The demand took me by surprise for two significant reasons. Firstly, a signed contract was already in place, with all terms agreed upon and finalised. Secondly, Sophia's history made the request even more perplexing. In 1982, she had made headlines after serving 17 days in prison in Italy for tax evasion—a charge for which she was ultimately cleared by the Supreme Court of Italy in 2013. The idea of such a prominent figure involving herself in an untraceable cash transaction seemed highly unlikely and raised serious doubts in my mind.

Adding to my unease, the Prince revealed that one of the preconditions for this transaction was complete secrecy—no one else was to know, not even my team or collaborators. The only other person aware of the situation was his brother, who had lent him the money to make the payment. The Prince assured me that he had already handled everything and that the funds had been paid directly to Sophia's manager. Though I wasn't happy about it, the deal was done, and my hands were tied. I had no choice but to move forward, despite my growing discomfort.

As the gala date approached, the Prince's calls became more frequent and insistent. He repeatedly brought up his brother, pressing me to ensure the money was repaid as soon as possible. The constant hassling added another layer of stress to an already fraught situation. I was juggling the immense pressure of organising a high-profile event while grappling with the uneasy feeling that something wasn't quite right. The urgency of his demands only deepened my doubts, but at that point, there was no turning back.

I desperately wanted this gala to be the talk of the town, a shining moment that would lift my profile and give me the fresh start I so desperately needed. It was my chance to prove myself, to show that I could overcome the setbacks and rise above the chaos. But the pressures I put on myself were immense, and I found myself surrounded by people whose focus was only on money—always demanding more and more.

The constant stress, the mounting demands, and the weight of trying to make everything perfect became unbearable. I felt trapped, spiralling deeper into a life I barely recognised. As the months went on, my escape became the gambling machines. They were the only place where I could shut off my thoughts, a refuge where I didn't have to face the reality of my life unravelling. For those fleeting moments in front of the machines, the flashing lights and hypnotic sounds dulled the pain. But in the back of my mind, I knew I was sinking further into despair, even as I tried to convince myself otherwise.

I won't dwell too much on the lead-up to the event, but suffice it to say that costs were skyrocketing, and it seemed like everyone wanted a piece of the action without putting any money into it. The pressure was immense, but when the night of the gala finally arrived, it was nothing short of spectacular.

The room was filled with some of the most prominent figures in Australia, including some of the nation's wealthiest individuals like Gina Rinehart and Lindsay Fox, to name just a few. It was a truly star-studded evening. I had the incredible opportunity to spend time with Sophia Loren, who was as stunning and gracious as I'd imagined.

The culinary experience was extraordinary—a 9-course degustation menu designed by an Italian chef who incorporated some of Australia's finest ingredients to create a truly Italian feast with a local twist. It was a celebration of the best of both worlds, blending Italian traditions with Australian excellence.

The entertainment was equally breathtaking, a fusion of Italian and Australian music. Some of Australia's most beloved artists graced the stage, including John Swan, Ray Burgess, Marty Rhone and John St Peeters, who brought the house down with their 'Legends of the Southern Land' theme. Phil Walley-Stack, an incredible Indigenous singer-songwriter, and Indigenous dancers added a heartfelt and powerful dimension to the evening. The atmosphere was electric, and for one unforgettable night, it felt like all the challenges and sacrifices had been worth it.

On the evening of the gala, I was thrilled to raise over $60,000 for the charity. It was a significant achievement, and knowing that the funds would go to support the Alannah & Madeline Foundation's mission to keep children safe from violence made it even more meaningful.

Sophia Loren's generosity added a special touch to the night. She donated one of her stunning Armani Privée gowns for the auction, which fetched an impressive $20,000. It was a true highlight and a testament to her grace and willingness to support the cause.

However, not everything went as planned. One of the auction items—a Maserati—failed to meet expectations, selling for just $2,000 above reserve. I had pinned so much hope on that car being a showstopper, imagining it would raise a far higher sum. Despite the disappointment, the charity was incredibly pleased with the overall outcome. They shared that the publicity generated by the event, especially with Sophia Loren's involvement, was worth far more to them than any single auction item. The exposure helped shine a spotlight on their mission, amplifying their reach and impact far beyond what we raised on the night.

While I had hoped for more, I took comfort in knowing that the event had accomplished something far greater than I had anticipated, leaving a lasting impression on a cause that was so close to my heart.

During the week that the Prince, Sophia, and her team were in Australia, something felt off. There was a sense of unease that I couldn't shake, as though pieces of the puzzle weren't fitting together. After they left, I decided to message Sophia's manager directly, politely asking if they could provide something in writing for my records regarding the €50,000 cash payment. To my utter surprise, the manager had no idea what I was talking about. He assured me that such a request had never been made, nor would it have been, as it was completely against their practice. He suggested I speak with the Prince for clarification.

This revelation left me reeling. It became clear that the Prince had been lying, fabricating a story about Sophia's management demanding the cash payment. He had gone out of his way to make it appear as though this was a legitimate request, adding layers of secrecy to ensure I wouldn't question it. Within ten minutes of my exchange with Sophia's manager, the Prince called me, his voice filled with anger. He demanded to know what I had done and ordered me to call the manager back, insisting I claim it was a misunderstanding on my part.

I stood my ground. I told him I would do no such thing. My refusal only fuelled his fury, and he angrily hung up on me. Not long after, I received an email from him. In it, he admitted that the €50,000 was actually his 'spotter's fee'—a detail he had intentionally hidden by concocting the lie about Sophia's management.

I was furious. At no stage had this so-called 'fee' been mentioned, let alone agreed upon. Feeling utterly betrayed, I emailed him back, demanding an explanation. I also questioned why I had been made to pay his friend €10,000 under the pretence of securing Sophia's involvement. The realisation that I had been so thoroughly deceived by someone I trusted was devastating. His secrecy, lies, and manipulation shattered whatever trust had remained.

After everything unfolded, I sought legal advice to see what could be done. While the lawyer acknowledged that I had a genuine case, they explained that dealing with Italian law would be a long and arduous process, taking years to make any headway, and even then, there were no guarantees of success. Faced with the daunting prospect of an endless legal battle, I decided to let it go. I stopped corresponding with the Prince entirely, determined to put this painful chapter behind me.

Three months later, out of the blue, I received a WhatsApp message from the Prince. He claimed to miss me, insisting that the whole ordeal had been a misunderstanding. He offered to provide first-class return tickets for my family and me, along with a home to stay in Rome, so that we could discuss the matter face to face and hopefully resolve it.

I didn't even consider accepting his offer. The thought of stepping foot in Italy under his arrangement was terrifying. I couldn't shake the fear that he might have orchestrated something sinister—perhaps even having me arrested upon arrival. My trust in him had been completely shattered. His message only reaffirmed my decision to cut ties with him and protect myself and my family from any further harm. I didn't trust him.

The entire experience was a painful lesson in misplaced trust and the high cost of compromise. It tested me in ways I never thought possible, forcing me to confront difficult truths and ultimately shaping my character. The emotional toll was staggering. I felt deeply betrayed by people I had trusted, manipulated into a web of deceit and false promises. Sleepless nights were consumed with frustration and disillusionment as the dream I had worked so tirelessly to build began unravelling before my eyes.

After everything I endured, my trust in dealing with Italians was reduced to zero. I swore to myself that I would never place my faith in them again. This chapter of my life, however painful, stands as a testament to resilience, integrity, and the pursuit of ambitious dreams in the face of adversity. It taught me invaluable lessons about navigating betrayal and finding strength amid turmoil—lessons that continue to guide me in everything I do.

Chapter 10

A New Direction

With my trust in Italians shattered, I knew I needed a fresh start. Determined to distance myself from the betrayals of the past, I sought the help of an American broker recommended by a friend to secure talent for my upcoming events in Australia. It was a leap of faith, but one rooted in cautious optimism that this new chapter would bring the stability I so desperately needed. I was determined to rebuild not just my business but my confidence, hoping that a shift in direction would allow me to rise from the ashes.

We began brainstorming ideas for Italian actors to headline my next big event in Australia. Naturally, Al Pacino and Robert De Niro were my top choices. Their star power and deep Italian heritage made them ideal candidates, but their fees were astronomical, far beyond my budget. Other names came up, but none of them had the cultural connection or magnetic appeal I sought to captivate an audience. Just when it felt like we were running out of options, Alec Baldwin's name surfaced.

At first, I hesitated. Alec wasn't Italian, and this event was meant to celebrate Italian culture. However, I discovered that Alec had been honoured with the prestigious Friend of Italy Award in 2014, recognising his connection to and appreciation of Italian culture. His global stardom, unmatched talent, and the novelty of this being his first visit to Australia made him the perfect choice. The buzz of excitement surrounding Alec's appearance was palpable, and the decision felt right.

I quickly signed a contract, ensuring Alec's participation. As was my tradition, I attached a charity to the event—this time, Bully Zero, an organisation committed to preventing bullying and cyberbullying in schools, workplaces, and communities across Australia. The cause resonated deeply with me, and Alec wholeheartedly embraced it. He appeared on TV, radio, and various media outlets, passionately promoting both the event and the charity.

However, the decision to feature Alec wasn't without controversy. Critics questioned why an event tied to Italian culture would feature someone who wasn't Italian. Others brought up his past controversies, including the infamous voicemail where he called his daughter a 'pig' during a bitter custody battle, as well as accusations of offensive remarks over the years. Headlines accused him of being polarising, referencing his history of controversial comments and behaviour.

Despite the backlash, I stood firm. 'We all make mistakes,' I explained to critics. 'None of us are perfect.' I acknowledged Alec's struggles, noting that the voicemail incident occurred during an emotionally charged divorce, a situation that could push anyone to their limits. I'd seen parents say far worse in moments of frustration, and I believed in giving people the space to grow and change. Over the years, Alec had proven himself as a talented actor and someone capable of leveraging his platform for good causes. I admired his resilience and talent and believed his participation could make a meaningful impact.

The excitement for Alec's first trip to Australia was undeniable. Fans eagerly anticipated the chance to meet him, and tickets to the event were selling quite well. On the surface, everything seemed perfect. My reputation as a successful businesswoman was intact. I personified confidence, competence, and success. But inside, I was falling apart. The weight of my personal struggles— mounting debts, a growing gambling addiction, and the fear of my secret life being exposed—was unbearable. This event wasn't just a professional venture; it was a lifeline. I needed it to succeed to maintain the image I had so carefully constructed.

During the Sophia Loren trip, I made friends with a chef from Sydney who shared my passion for creating memorable culinary experiences. After the event, we stayed in touch, exchanging ideas and supporting each other's work. When he heard about my plans for the Alec Baldwin Gala, he was immediately excited. Alec is a vegan, and we knew that designing a menu to suit his preferences while maintaining the elegance expected of such a prestigious event would be both a creative challenge and an exciting opportunity. Together, we began brainstorming ideas for a vegan menu that would meet Alec's high standards and impress our distinguished guests.

To bring our vision to life, I introduced him to the Italian chef who had designed the menu for the Sophia Loren event, as well as an award-winning chef based in Melbourne. With their combined expertise, they worked together to create a menu that not only catered to Alec's tastes but also elevated the entire experience. This collaboration set the foundation for what was shaping up to be one of the most ambitious events I had ever worked on.

The gala wasn't just about food; it was about crafting an experience that embodied Hollywood glamour while honouring the late summer season. The chefs and I made an important decision early on: every item on the menu, from the finger food to the desserts, would be gluten-free. This practical choice ensured we could accommodate all dietary needs without the risk of last-minute surprises. Designing gluten-free dishes that were also vegan and still full of flavour and elegance required extra thought and care, but it was a challenge we embraced wholeheartedly.

The logistics of the kitchen were another challenge. After much discussion, we decided to use the Crown Casino's kitchen, specifically requesting their pastry chefs. Their work on the Sophia Loren dessert at a previous event had been flawless. If our pastry chef from Italy couldn't make it, I knew they'd be up to the task of creating vegan desserts that would leave a lasting impression.

Our menu was all about the 'wow factor.' It was Hollywood-inspired, yet perfectly suited to the Australian summer. Every detail was deliberate:

- Three types of vegan canapés to kick things off.

- Antipasto plates brimming with seasonal produce.

- Entrées featuring three exquisite vegan items on a single plate.

- Main courses offering refined vegan alternatives to traditional dishes.

- Desserts—a trio of perfectly balanced vegan treats to end the evening on a high note.

We consciously avoided pasta and lobster. Pasta didn't feel right for such an elevated event, and lobster, while luxurious, wasn't suitable for a vegan menu. The last thing we wanted was for a beautiful dish to arrive at the table cold and uninspiring.

Alongside the gala, we also planned a private dinner for Alec Baldwin the evening before. That menu, while more intimate, had to match the level of excellence we aimed to deliver for the gala itself.

Looking back, the Alec Baldwin Gala wasn't just about creating a meal; it was about telling a story through food—one that reflected Alec's vegan values, the glamour of Hollywood, the freshness of an Australian summer, and the passion of a team committed to excellence. These moments—these challenges and triumphs—reminded me why I loved what I do.

Meanwhile, following the success of my event with Sophia Loren, my reputation within the industry continued to flourish. In December 2015, I received an unexpected call from a Melbourne-based legal firm that also operated as a talent agency with offices in the U.S. They wanted to know if I was interested in organising an event for none other than Goldie Hawn in Australia.

The opportunity to work with such a Hollywood icon was thrilling. I quickly arranged a meeting to discuss the brief and, after reviewing their requirements, submitted a detailed quote. Unfortunately, the event didn't materialise. However, the conversation wasn't a total loss. The firm assured me that if I ever needed talent for future events, they'd be delighted to collaborate. It was a promising connection, and I felt a sense of validation knowing my work was garnering attention from such high-profile players.

During our meeting, I mentioned that I had already secured Alec Baldwin through a U.S. broker back in August 2015. They seemed impressed and encouraged me to keep them in mind for future projects. Although the Goldie Hawn event didn't come to fruition, it served as another reminder of how one successful event could open doors to new opportunities and connections.

With Alec Baldwin confirmed and the event set for February 27, 2016, I poured every ounce of my energy into making it a success. The stakes were higher than ever. This wasn't just about Alec, the charity, or the event itself— it was about keeping my world intact and proving, if only to myself, that I could overcome the chaos and create something extraordinary.

At first, everything seemed to be going well. The event was generating buzz, and Alec's appearance was drawing significant attention. However, things took an unexpected turn when Alec came across a couple of negative media articles about him. The criticism clearly struck a nerve, but what escalated the situation was a comment made by the CEO of Bully Zero, the charity we had partnered with for the event.

The CEO had a tendency to shoot his mouth off, and this time was no exception. He publicly remarked on Alec's past controversies, perhaps intending to address the media backlash, but his words didn't sit well with Alec. To my frustration, Alec decided to call the CEO directly to confront him. I was caught off guard and annoyed by the situation. The CEO shouldn't have made such remarks, especially since Alec's involvement was significantly boosting the charity's visibility. At the same time, Alec's direct approach complicated things. I was funding his trip, but I felt that, out of professionalism, he should have addressed the matter through me instead of engaging with the CEO directly.

It was an uncomfortable situation that threatened to overshadow all the work I had put into the event. I found myself stuck in the middle, mediating between Alec and the charity while trying to keep the event on track. It was yet another reminder of how quickly things could unravel when working with high-profile individuals and organisations.

I remember the day vividly—26 January 2016. It was my mum and dad's 60th wedding anniversary, and we were in Sydney celebrating this incredible milestone as a family. In the middle of the festivities, I received a phone call from the broker that Alec Baldwin had pulled out of the event. No reason was given. The news hit me like a freight train—I collapsed under the weight of it. The event was only a month away. What was I meant to do? There was no way I could replace him after all the media hype.

In my panic, I called my PR company in tears, desperate for guidance. They advised me to keep everything under wraps until we had official confirmation in writing. For days, I held on to a glimmer of hope that maybe it wasn't true, but on February 2, I received a WhatsApp message from the broker that shattered those hopes. It read, 'At an event in London, but despite all of my best efforts, Alec will be cancelling the event.' I couldn't believe it. I was devastated and furious at the same time.

I immediately told the broker I needed everything in writing within the hour, or I would seek legal advice. He responded that Alec's team was preparing a formal statement, but to this day, I have never seen it. Then, the broker added insult to injury by suggesting he could quickly secure Andy Garcia for the same price. While I respected Andy Garcia as an actor, I couldn't justify the connection—apart from his role in *The Godfather*, he had no ties to Italy. It didn't fit the event's theme, and it felt like a desperate attempt to placate me.

Determined not to let this betrayal slide, I contacted the legal firm in Melbourne for advice on recovering not just the fees I had paid for Alec, but also the significant expenses I had incurred for PR and marketing. They assured me they would get my money back and even promised they could secure a big Italian name, such as Al Pacino, for the same fee. It sounded like a lifeline.

The firm sent a formal letter to the broker demanding a full refund, but he outright refused. In response, legal action was initiated in the United States. However, what I didn't realise at the time was that the firm didn't have a legal office in the U.S.—they were working through a third party. This revelation added another layer of complication to an already chaotic situation.

Ultimately, I had no choice but to cancel the event. I was forced to face the media and share the truth—that Alec had cancelled, and to this day, I still don't know the reason why. It was a devastating blow, both professionally and personally.

The court case proceeded in the U.S., and while I won, the victory was hollow. The broker had no money or assets to his name, making it impossible to recover the funds. To this day, I have not seen a cent of the money I invested, and the entire ordeal remains one of the most bitter chapters of my career.

The fallout was unbearable. With everything spiralling out of control, I felt utterly alone, ashamed, and embarrassed. I couldn't bring myself to talk to anyone about it. The mounting pressure, coupled with my overwhelming sense of failure, drove me further into gambling. It was my only escape, the only place where I could temporarily shut out the chaos of my life. But with gambling came more stealing, and with every stolen dollar and every bet placed, the hole I was in grew deeper. On top of that, I was still paying legal fees and other expenses to people who weren't delivering results.

The entire ordeal left me feeling broken—financially, emotionally, and morally. I had no idea how I would climb out of the wreckage.

There were countless moments when I thought about ending it all, about escaping the relentless pain and the crushing weight of my failures. The shame, the guilt, and the overwhelming sense of hopelessness made it feel like there was no way out. I can't even count how many times I came to the edge, ready to take my life and put an end to the torment.

But every time, something—something I couldn't quite define—held me back. Maybe it was a faint glimmer of hope buried deep within, or maybe it was the thought of the people I would leave behind. I'll never fully understand what it was, but at the very last moment, I would always change my mind. Something, someone, or maybe just the tiniest shred of resilience within me, kept me going.

While the legal battle over Alec Baldwin's cancellation raged on in the U.S., the legal and talent firm in Melbourne and I began exploring new possibilities for a replacement. Al Pacino was still out of reach financially, so we went through a list of other names, trying to find someone with similar star power. Eventually, I settled on Susan Sarandon. I had always admired her—not only for her incredible body of work but also for her outspoken activism and unwavering authenticity. She seemed like the perfect choice.

To my relief, Susan accepted our offer. This would mark her first visit to Australia, and the timing felt serendipitous—it coincided with the 25th anniversary of her iconic film *Thelma & Louise*. Inspired by the milestone, I decided to change both the event date and format. Instead of hosting a single event, I planned a leadership luncheon featuring Susan, followed by *An Evening with Susan Sarandon*. The new concept felt fresh and exciting, and I was determined to make it a success.

Securing the funds for Susan's visit was another hurdle. I had no choice but to ask my husband to refinance the mortgage on our home, so I could cover the costs. It was a difficult conversation, but I assured him that once the US court case was resolved or the Susan Sarandon events turned a profit, I would pay it back. It wasn't an easy decision, but I believed this was my chance to redeem myself financially despite everything I had been through.

While working on Susan's event, the legal firm revisited the idea of hosting Goldie Hawn in Australia. According to them, Goldie was eager to visit, and they proposed a fifty-fifty partnership for the event. Although tempting, I had to decline—I was already financially overextended with Susan's event, and Goldie didn't align with the Italian theme I had been curating for my events. I hoped my explanation would put the matter to rest.

However, when I mentioned this to the Sydney chef, he expressed interest in collaborating with me on this event. I explained that I didn't have any funds to go forward, but he said that he would initially fund it from money that he had inherited money from his grandmother. Upon the sale of the tickets, he would be the first one paid off. It was an unexpected but welcome solution.

We agreed to model Goldie's event after Susan's: a leadership luncheon and *An Evening with Goldie Hawn*. As a gesture of goodwill, we decided to donate a portion of the luncheon funds to Goldie's charity, MindUp. To manage the project, the chef and I formed a new company together, and I covered the upfront costs for the setup and used my office and equipment as the base. With the contract signed, we moved forward with confidence.

Soon after, my partner received a call from the legal firm explaining Goldie had an additional condition: $100,000 needed to be guaranteed for MindUp before she would participate in the luncheon. This was frustrating, as the luncheon was already part of the signed contract, and the charity's benefit had initially been a goodwill gesture. The firm reassured us ticket sales would cover the $100,000, so my partner agreed—on the condition the funds would be paid after ticket sales were finalised. The firm agreed.

A week later, the legal firm informed us Goldie now required the $100,000 to be held in their trust account before committing. Although this was unexpected, my partner transferred the money, trusting the legal firm's assurances that the funds would be secure and used solely for this purpose. The project moved forward.

Meanwhile, I was juggling the Susan Sarandon event, scheduled for early August, and Goldie's events, planned for November. Balancing these massive projects left me exhausted, but I remained determined to make them both a success. The stakes were higher than ever—I needed these events to stabilise my business and redeem myself.

Managing Susan's event came with its own challenges. Communication was cumbersome, as all messages were filtered through the legal firm in Melbourne—I wasn't allowed to speak directly with Susan. Instead, everything had to go through this third party, which made the process tiresome and tedious. The female lawyer I was dealing with was particularly controlling, which added another layer of difficulty.

Also, everything this woman touched seemed to turn to dust. For someone in the legal profession, she failed to cross her t's or dot her i's. One glaring issue arose with Getty Images regarding the pricing she had committed to. She had one understanding of the agreement, while Getty had another, and the resulting confusion cost me a fortune.

I had secured Crown Casino as a sponsor for Susan's accommodation, but according to the lawyer, Susan refused to stay there, opting for the Grand Hyatt instead. This change added unnecessary costs that I was already struggling to manage. Hoping to offset these expenses, I approached L'Oréal, a brand Susan was an ambassador for, to become a sponsor. Unfortunately, they declined. While these setbacks were discouraging, I was determined to push forward.

My PR team was feeling the strain as well, struggling with the lack of responses we were receiving. Desperate for help, I hired an 'event negotiator' who came highly recommended by my network. During our initial meeting, she exuded confidence and reliability, presenting herself as someone who could deliver results under pressure. However, her contributions ended up being minimal. She managed to source a few gifts for Susan and distributed some of the event passes to her connections, which I had permitted.

Unfortunately, I didn't have the time or energy to dwell on her shortcomings. When she explained that the limited timeframe had prevented her from achieving more, I chose to believe her and pressed on. There was no room for delays or distractions—I had to focus on making the event a success.

One of Australia's major TV stations came on board as a media sponsor for Susan's event, requiring exclusivity for all interviews. As part of their sponsorship, they provided an entertainment presenter to act as the MC for both the leadership luncheon and the evening event. The presenter was also scheduled to interview Susan at their Melbourne studio, adding valuable media exposure to the event.

A week before Susan's events, I received an email from the legal firm in Melbourne requesting my approval for a L'Oréal proposal. They wanted Susan to attend a small influencer luncheon in Sydney on the 8th, following my Melbourne events. The luncheon was described as an exclusive, 30-person Q&A session with influencers and key media to discuss the L'Oréal products Susan endorses.

I found this request both confronting and unacceptable. As part of my agreement with Susan, I held full exclusivity to her appearances in Australia for 30 days prior to and 30 days after my event. This exclusivity was non-negotiable and critical to the success of my event. Allowing Susan to participate in another engagement, especially for a company that had declined to sponsor my event, was completely out of the question.

Somehow, I couldn't shake the feeling that this was orchestrated. It seemed like L'Oréal had planned this as soon as they learned Susan was coming to Australia, waiting until the last minute to raise the issue in the hope that I would feel pressured to agree. The timing and approach felt strategic, designed to bully me into bending to their demands.

There was no way I was going to approve this. The exclusivity clause was in place for a reason—to ensure that my event retained its unique value and that Susan's presence wasn't diluted by other engagements. I immediately rejected the proposal, making it clear that this request not only violated the terms of our agreement but also showed a lack of respect for the work and investment I had put into organising her visit.

The entire situation left me questioning the transparency of the legal firm and whether they were acting in my best interest—or if their loyalty lay elsewhere. It was yet another hurdle in an already complicated and stressful project, but I refused to compromise on what I had worked so hard to achieve.

Excited to finally meet Susan, I planned to greet her personally at the airport. However, the legal firm strongly advised against it, insisting she would be too tired after her flight. Later, I was told I could meet her in the hotel lobby instead. I waited there for over an hour, but she never appeared. Frustrated,

I eventually left, only to discover later on Instagram that Susan had spent the afternoon exploring Melbourne, visiting galleries, and purchasing art. Her disregard for our scheduled meeting was infuriating.

The day of the luncheon arrived with significant media coverage and an incredible guest list, including Dannii Minogue, Turia Pitt, Janine Allis, Em Rusciano, and many others. The atmosphere was electric, but Susan's late arrival—nearly two hours after the scheduled start time—left guests and media visibly frustrated. The delay disrupted the carefully planned timeline and added an air of discomfort to what should have been a seamless event.

Adding to the tension, Susan's tardiness garnered bad publicity. One fan commented on her Instagram account, calling her out for being almost two hours late to the luncheon and describing her behaviour as rude. Susan replied publicly, claiming she wasn't late—she had arrived at the luncheon when she was told to. While her response deflected responsibility, it only added fuel to the fire and highlighted the miscommunication behind the scenes.

As if that wasn't enough, the MC compounded the chaos. Slurring his words during the luncheon, he handed me the microphone mid-event and announced he wouldn't be staying to MC the evening program, as he had decided to fly back to Sydney instead. Scrambling to find a replacement, I managed to secure someone at the last minute, but the stress of the day was overwhelming. What should have been a celebration of excellence had turned into a series of challenges I had to navigate on the fly.

The evening show eventually came and went. The theatre was full, but only because a significant number of tickets had been given away due to poor sales. After the event, Susan was scheduled for a meet-and-greet with 50 guests upstairs. While I initially aimed for 100 guests, the request was declined. Susan was gracious with those who attended, but my personal interaction with her remained minimal, leaving a sense of unfinished business.

The Sydney chef, who had attended the luncheon, sensed the tension underlying the event. When we met the following day, my emotions finally overflowed. I broke down, pouring out my frustrations about the legal team's controlling behaviour and the endless hurdles I faced. He listened with genuine concern, acknowledging the gravity of the issues. Troubled by my experience, he drafted a detailed letter outlining critical questions and concerns about the upcoming Goldie Hawn event, hoping to prevent similar problems.

Reflecting on the sequence of events, I couldn't shake the feeling that the challenges with Susan's visit weren't coincidental. The legal team's orchestration of last-minute requests—such as the L'Oréal influencer luncheon—seemed calculated to push boundaries and test my resolve. It wasn't just a misunderstanding; it felt like deliberate manoeuvring, which added an unnecessary layer of strain to an already challenging project.

By the time Susan's events concluded, I was mentally and emotionally drained. Despite the media buzz and celebrity glamour, the experience left me questioning the integrity of the partnerships I had relied on. These were hard-earned lessons, and as I turned my focus to the Goldie Hawn event, I knew I needed to take greater control. However, even with those precautions, nothing could have prepared me for the nightmare that lay ahead.

Chapter 11

Betrayal and Grace

Fresh from the rollercoaster of Susan Sarandon's events, I approached the planning phase for Goldie Hawn with a mix of cautious optimism and lingering anxiety. Susan's events had pushed me to my limits, exposing gaps in communication, trust, and management that I vowed to address. I told myself that the lessons learned would make me stronger, better equipped to navigate the complexities of another high-profile event. Yet, as I stood at the threshold of this new challenge, I had no inkling of what lay ahead. The challenges awaiting me would make Susan's event seem like a mere warm-up act.

Looking back, I sometimes wonder if I had an invisible sign plastered across my forehead that read 'Sucker' or 'Loser.' Time and again, I seemed to attract leeches—people who were all too eager to exploit my goodwill, tenacity, and unyielding determination to succeed. Whether it was controlling legal teams, opportunistic partners, or impossible client demands, I often found myself trapped in a web of others' agendas, my own voice drowned out by their louder, more insistent ones.

The issues with the Goldie Hawn project began almost immediately. Despite having a signed contract and an agreed timeline, cracks began to show. Communication breakdowns, sudden demands, and unanticipated obstacles piled up like storm clouds on the horizon. The legal team, which had already proven challenging during Susan's events, resumed their pattern of control. They frequently bypassed me, making decisions without my input and treating me more like an observer than the producer. It was infuriating and disempowering.

As soon as Susan's events concluded, my Sydney partner wasted no time in raising concerns about the Goldie Hawn project. His email to the legal firm was meticulous, addressing issues that mirrored my own frustrations. This time, the stakes were higher, and it wasn't just about logistics. It was about transparency, financial accountability, and ensuring everyone's roles were clearly defined to avoid missteps.

One of his key concerns was financial clarity. He requested a comprehensive statement from the Legal Trust Account to verify that the funds he had transferred—$100,000 on May 5th, $90,784 on May 6th, and another $100,000 on June 13th—had been properly allocated for the Goldie Hawn Production and Leadership Luncheon. Additionally, he asked for a company letterhead to document these amounts as loans to the company. The level of detail in his request underscored the seriousness of the situation. It wasn't just about trust anymore; it was about safeguarding the integrity of the project and ensuring accountability.

Another concern was the inexplicable delay in announcing Goldie's event. We had been told we couldn't make any announcements until Susan's event was over—a strategy that seemed counterintuitive. The more time we had to promote, the better our chances of selling out. Susan's event had already demonstrated how delays in approvals could hurt ticket sales, even with an expensive marketing campaign. It was frustrating to see history repeating itself.

His email received little response from the legal firm, which by now had become a predictable and infuriating pattern. By late September, with the event scheduled for mid-November, time was slipping away. There were no announcements, no marketing, and no clear direction. The lack of cooperation from the legal team left me increasingly uneasy. Together with the event negotiator, I decided to dig deeper to uncover who was truly managing Goldie Hawn's involvement.

To our shock, the name we had been given as Goldie's representative led nowhere. The more we searched, the clearer it became that something was seriously amiss.

Amid this growing confusion, I was approached by a local charity with questions about Goldie Hawn's involvement in Melbourne. At first, I thought they were simply curious about the logistics or perhaps interested in collaborating. But as we spoke, their questions became more pointed, and I sensed there was a deeper story unfolding. They wanted to know how I had managed to secure Goldie, considering their own experience with the same legal firm managing my event. What they revealed was as shocking as it was disheartening.

The charity explained that they had worked with the same legal firm months earlier on a project to bring Goldie to Melbourne. They had poured significant resources into the endeavour, dedicating countless hours to securing her involvement and planning the event. They had even engaged another event manager to oversee the logistics. However, the legal firm ultimately reneged on the deal, leaving the charity with nothing to show for their hard work. The team was devastated—not only had they wasted precious time and funds, but their trust in the process had been shattered.

Hearing their account, I couldn't help but feel a pang of anger and sympathy. For a charity, where every dollar counts, such a setback was not just a financial blow but also an emotional one. It was infuriating to think that the same firm creating havoc in my project had left another organisation grappling with disappointment and loss.

They mentioned the event manager they had worked with, and to my surprise, I recognised the name—it was a colleague I had crossed paths with in the industry. Determined to learn more, I reached out to her directly to hear her side of the story. What she shared only deepened my concern.

The event manager confirmed the charity's account, adding further details about how the legal firm's actions had derailed the project. She described how the firm had initially seemed committed to the event, only to backtrack on their promises when it came time to deliver. The charity's funds, time, and trust had been squandered, leaving her in a precarious position as well. Her frustration was palpable, and I could hear the distress in her voice as she recounted the ordeal.

The more I learned, the more unsettling the picture became. This wasn't an isolated incident; it seemed to be a pattern. The legal firm's actions were leaving a trail of broken promises and dashed hopes, damaging not only businesses but also charities that depended on integrity and professionalism to achieve their goals. It was both infuriating and heartbreaking.

This knowledge weighed heavily on me. I couldn't shake the sense of responsibility—not for the legal firm's actions, of course, but for ensuring that my event with Goldie didn't become another entry in their history of failures. The stakes felt even higher now—not just for me, but for everyone who had suffered because of their unethical behaviour. It strengthened my resolve to see the luncheon through, not just for my own reputation but to prove that integrity could prevail, even in the face of such adversity.

Determined to get answers, I reached out to Alan Nevins, Goldie's Literary and Talent Manager in the United States, confident that if anyone could clarify what was happening, it would be him.

When we introduced ourselves and mentioned Goldie's supposed trip to Australia, Alan's response was startling. He had no idea what we were talking about. No event, no dates, no plans—nothing had been discussed or approved. However, he suggested it might involve her charity, MindUp, and promised to reach out to Goldie directly for clarification. His willingness to assist was a small ray of hope amid the growing storm.

Hours later, Alan called back with even more alarming news. Goldie had been approached about a potential trip to Australia, but the details were vague. She knew nothing about the specifics of the event, the dates, or the $100,000 donation allegedly designated for her charity. She was as baffled as we were and promised to speak with MindUp's CEO to investigate further. Alan assured us that Goldie would get in touch once she had more information.

When Goldie finally called, her revelations were both shocking and disheartening. Not only was she unaware of the charity luncheon, but the Melbourne legal firm's U.S. representative also confirmed that no such funds had been received from their Melbourne office. It was October, and with the event scheduled for November 14, we were left scrambling to salvage what we could.

As if the external chaos weren't enough, the internal pressure at the office with my business partner added another layer of stress. My partner, understandably furious about the missing $100,000, wouldn't stop going on and on about it. His frustration was relentless, and while I understood his anger, it drove me absolutely nuts. Every day, I had to deal with his questions and accusations, as if repeating them might somehow conjure the money back. Even his lawyer eventually stepped in, advising him to calm down and let the event play out before deciding on our next steps. While I appreciated the lawyer's practical advice, it did little to ease the tension at home. The constant pressure compounded my already overwhelming stress and made me feel like I was battling on multiple fronts—professionally, personally, and emotionally.

At the same time, I found myself sinking deeper and deeper into gambling. The stress of dealing with the legal firm's mismanagement, the mounting financial burdens, and the relentless pressure to keep the event afloat became overwhelming. Gambling had started as a distraction, a way to escape the chaos, but it quickly spiralled out of control. I began stealing more money from my client—not just to cover event costs but also to fund my gambling. Every time I thought I could win enough to make things right, I dug myself into an even deeper hole. The shame and guilt were consuming, but the cycle was impossible to break as the pressures around me mounted.

Faced with mounting chaos, we had no choice but to hire a lawyer to address the fiasco caused by the female lawyer managing the project. The investigation revealed shocking truths: she had misappropriated funds from the trust account, forged the chef's signature, and manipulated key stakeholders. These revelations felt like the final blow to an already fragile situation.

Despite the turmoil, Goldie's grace and professionalism shone through. She agreed to honour the luncheon, even without the promised donation to her charity. Rather than cancelling, we reframed the event as a showcase for MindUp, creating an opportunity for Goldie to connect with influential Australians and lay the groundwork for establishing her charity in the country.

Securing a venue sponsor became our lifeline. We managed to secure one of Melbourne's most prestigious locations, ensuring the event could proceed without incurring additional costs. However, the lawyer's sabotage continued—her team falsely claimed to Goldie's representatives that the venue was substandard. Anticipating such tactics, I had prepared detailed information and photos of the venue, proving its status as a top-rated location. This proactive step reassured Goldie's team and kept the event on track.

The luncheon, scaled down to an intimate gathering of forty distinguished guests, became a testament to resilience and adaptability. Senators, ministers, educators, and select celebrities, including Anthony from The Wiggles, were part of a carefully curated guest list. The smaller scale created an atmosphere of warmth and exclusivity, allowing Goldie to engage personally with each attendee. She answered questions, posed for photos, and left a lasting impression on everyone in the room.

Adding a personal touch, we discovered it was Goldie's birthday. Determined to make it special, I arranged for a beautiful birthday cake and a heartfelt rendition of 'Happy Birthday' by a talented Melbourne singer. The event negotiator organised thoughtful gifts from her friends, adding to the celebratory atmosphere. Goldie embraced the festivities with joy, transforming the luncheon into a magical day.

Amidst the celebration, the shadow of deceit still lingered. Goldie revealed she had been told the luncheon was scheduled for 1:30 p.m., not 12:00 p.m. This deliberate miscommunication mirrored the confusion caused during Susan Sarandon's visit, where the same lawyer had provided false information. Both women had joked about the odd timing, asking, 'Who has lunch at 1:30 p.m.?' These lies had created unnecessary stress, highlighting the manipulative tactics at play.

The marketing efforts—or lack thereof—added another layer of frustration. Despite promises of a robust campaign, ticket prices were slashed without approval, and sales suffered. Opportunities for high-profile media coverage and interviews with Goldie were either blocked or never materialised, leaving us scrambling to fill seats.

A Night of Laughs with Goldie was warmly received by Melbourne and its audience. The event brought a sense of joy and connection that seemed to transcend the chaos that had preceded it. Goldie was, as always, incredible— gracious, engaging, and effortlessly charming. She had a way of making everyone feel seen and valued, and my partner and I were no exception. Both during the luncheon earlier in the day and that evening at the show, she made us feel warm and fuzzy, a rare gift amidst the stress and tension that had dominated the lead-up to this moment.

The same could not be said about the legal firm. Their behaviour throughout the process had been horrendous, to put it mildly. Every interaction with them was a struggle, riddled with evasiveness, miscommunication, and a complete lack of accountability. By this point, my patience with them had worn thin. Their involvement cast a shadow over what should have been an entirely celebratory occasion.

While the evening was a success, our time with Goldie was unfortunately limited. Apart from the luncheon earlier in the day and a quick photo shoot at the evening event, we didn't get to spend much time with her. Nevertheless, my partner and I were deeply grateful for Goldie's unwavering professionalism and warmth. She went above and beyond to ensure the event's success, even as the challenges we faced threatened to derail it at every turn.

After the event, I received a beautiful email from Goldie that touched me deeply. She wrote:

'I want to share with you as well that my experience in Melbourne was just fantastic. Everything went so smoothly and the luncheon you arranged and produced was perfection. I had a wonderful time and met some very empathetic and like-minded people. It was a joy. Thank you for caring and being such a lovely host.'

Her words were a balm for my weary soul, a reminder that amidst all the chaos, something truly meaningful had been achieved. It was a moment of validation, one that reinforced my belief in the power of connection and the importance of perseverance.

But unfortunately, the story didn't end there. After the event, the legal firm outright refused to reimburse us for the ticket sales we had covered, despite their clear obligation to do so. This left us no choice but to embark on a lengthy and gruelling legal battle to recover the funds. By the time the final payment was grudgingly made in December, we had spent over $80,000 in legal fees, fighting this firm at every step of the way.

We wanted to exit the contract, but doing so would have come at an even greater cost—there would be no refund of our money. With no viable alternative, we had to push forward, salvaging whatever we could from the wreckage. Every decision felt like walking a tightrope, balancing the need to protect what little we had left while navigating the legal and logistical chaos created by the firm.

The ordeal was not just financially draining—it was emotionally exhausting. Every step felt like an uphill battle, and while we ultimately managed to recover some of the money, my business partner never got back the full amount he was owed. To make matters worse, I was responsible for covering half of the loss, a devastating blow, especially since I had already lost money on the Susan Sarandon event. On top of that, the $175,000 I had borrowed from my husband to keep things afloat was now a debt that wouldn't be repaid to him.

This realisation was crushing. The strain on our relationship was undeniable—every conversation seemed to revolve around the money, and I could see the frustration and disappointment in his eyes. I tried to focus on salvaging what I could from the wreckage, but the weight of the debt and the emotional toll of my choices made it impossible to escape the guilt. My days became a whirlwind of stress and sleepless nights, trying to figure out how to fix what felt irreparably broken. It wasn't just my finances unravelling, but also my sense of self-worth and responsibility as a partner.

Reflecting on the experience, I felt a mix of exhaustion, pride, and bittersweet relief. The event had succeeded in its own way, introducing MindUp to Australia and leaving a lasting impression on its attendees. Yet, the betrayal and manipulation by the legal team left a bitter taste, serving as a stark reminder of the importance of vigilance, accountability, and ethical leadership.

The Goldie Hawn event, initially envisioned as a career-defining moment, became a defining trial by fire. It tested my resilience and resolve, forcing me to confront the darker side of the industry while holding onto the values that mattered most. The lessons learned—about trust, adaptability, and the unyielding pursuit of excellence—became an indelible part of my journey, shaping the way I approached every project moving forward.

Even as I carried the weight of these challenges, I couldn't ignore the moments of light that emerged. Goldie's kind words, the connections forged at the luncheon, and the impact of introducing MindUp to a new audience reminded me why I had chosen this path in the first place. This chapter of my life wasn't just about setbacks; it was about finding strength in adversity and rediscovering the purpose that would guide me toward the next stage of my journey.

Chapter 12

Rebuilding Amidst Ruins

As the dust settled from the chaos of the Susan Sarandon and Goldie Hawn events, I found myself standing at a crossroads. The experience had tested every ounce of my resolve, leaving me financially depleted, emotionally drained, and questioning everything I thought I knew about the industry—and myself. Yet, somewhere amidst the rubble, there was a flicker of determination, a stubborn refusal to let these setbacks define my story.

Whilst juggling the complexities of the Susan Sarandon and Goldie Hawn events, I was also pouring my energy into creating something entirely new for Melbourne and Australia: Carnevale Australia. Inspired by the 800-year-old Venetian tradition, this event was a bold attempt to bring the magic, elegance, and cultural richness of Venice's iconic Carnevale to life in a modern and uniquely Australian way.

Venice has always held a special place in my heart. The charm of its winding canals, the grandeur of its architecture, and the magic of its Carnevale celebrations have captivated me for as long as I can remember. It had been a dream of mine to bring the vibrant and theatrical spirit of Carnevale to Melbourne—a celebration that combined elegance, history, and a sense of wonder. In 2017, that dream became a reality, though it was born not just out of passion but also out of purpose.

On August 24, 2016, a devastating 6.2 magnitude earthquake struck central Italy, reducing homes to rubble and forever changing the lives of its residents. The hill town of Amatrice bore the brunt of the disaster, with 299 lives lost and nearly 400 people injured. The destruction extended beyond Amatrice, causing widespread damage to the regions of Lazio, Marche, Umbria, and Abruzzo. Images of the devastation were heart-wrenching: families torn apart, entire communities flattened, and a centuries-old cultural heritage shaken to its core.

Those images haunted me, sparking an urgent desire to help. That's when Carnevale Australia was born—a two-week celebration of great food, music, and culture, designed to honour the Venetian tradition while raising funds for those affected by the disaster.

Melbourne was set to transform into a hub of Carnevale festivities, embracing an 800-year-old tradition with a modern twist. Party-goers would experience the best the city had to offer, but there was one requirement: everyone had to dress to impress, complete with a mask.

The highlight of the festival was the Masquerade Ball, a spectacular evening held on February 11, 2017, to officially launch the two-week Carnevale Australia festival. With the theme of 'Amore'—love—it was perfectly aligned with Valentine's Day, just three days later. This event promised to capture the romance and elegance of Venetian Carnevale, offering attendees a three-course meal, mesmerising entertainment, and the chance to revel in a night of glamour, passion, and purpose.

The ball served as the centrepiece of the festival, embodying the spirit of Carnevale while carrying a deeper message: party with a conscience to aid the victims of the devastating earthquake in Amatrice. The evening wasn't just about celebration—it was about making a difference, with every detail carefully planned to ensure it would be unforgettable.

The evening's success extended beyond the glamour and entertainment—it achieved its purpose in a profoundly meaningful way. Through the silent auction, raffle, and generous donations from attendees, the event raised over $41,000 for the victims of the devastating earthquake in central Italy. To ensure transparency and proper allocation, the funds were channelled through CO.AS.IT, an established organisation with deep ties to the Italian community. This partnership provided the assurance that every dollar would reach the people and regions most in need, bringing relief and hope to those who had lost so much.

The outpouring of generosity was humbling. Attendees didn't just come to celebrate—they came to make a difference. Each contribution, no matter the size, represented a shared commitment to support the rebuilding efforts and honour the resilience of the affected communities. The success of this fundraising effort reaffirmed the power of coming together, and it reminded me why events like these hold such transformative potential.

While this dream gave me something to work toward, the road ahead wasn't going to be easy. The aftermath of the Goldie Hawn event had left scars—financially, emotionally, and professionally. There were debts to repay, trust to rebuild, and a lingering sense of guilt that weighed heavily on my shoulders. My gambling had spiralled further out of control during the whirlwind of the last few months, and now, with no events on the horizon, the silence was deafening.

The financial strain was unrelenting. I owed my husband $175,000 from money I had borrowed to keep things afloat. My business partner had yet to recover from the losses incurred, and I was responsible for half of them. The emotional toll was just as heavy. Every missed payment and every failed promise felt like another crack in the foundation of my life.

I was haunted by the choices I had made—not just professionally but personally—and the realisation that I had to face the consequences, no matter how painful, was inescapable.

Amid this chaos, the vision of Carnevale Australia became my anchor. It was a chance to redeem myself, to channel my energy into something meaningful and restorative. I knew it wouldn't be enough to erase my mistakes, but it was a start. This project wasn't just about raising funds or creating an unforgettable event—it was about rebuilding, one step at a time, and proving to myself that I could rise again.

With the blessing of the Italian Consul General, we launched preparations for what would be a two-week celebration of Venetian tradition, culture, and style in the second half of 2017. To give the event the gravitas it deserved, I extended invitations at the end of August 2016 to several prominent individuals to join the event's advisory board. This board was carefully curated to include experts in PR, marketing, sponsorships, branding, and the arts. Their role was to help shape the event and leverage their networks to secure sponsorships and sell tables.

With a PR and marketing company on board, the promotion of Carnevale Australia began in earnest. The concept immediately captured attention, generating significant media interest and setting the stage for something truly spectacular. Melbourne was buzzing with curiosity about this Venetian-inspired festival, and I was determined to deliver an event that would leave people talking for years.

Despite the excitement and early momentum, challenges quickly arose. While the Italian Consul General threw himself into the project with enthusiasm, successfully selling tables and securing several small sponsors, the same could not be said for the rest of the advisory board. Despite their prominent roles and connections, the board members didn't sell a single ticket. This lack of engagement was frustrating, but I knew the event's success ultimately rested on my shoulders.

I decided against securing a big-name celebrity for the February launch of Carnevale, knowing that I didn't have the funds or the time required to attract sufficient sponsorships. Instead, I focused on making every detail extraordinary, confident that delivering a truly unforgettable experience would allow the reputation of Carnevale Australia to establish itself. Without the pressure to secure an Italian icon for February, I could prioritise building momentum and creating excitement for the November gala.

At the same time, I envisioned elevating the November gala to something extraordinary by bringing a Hollywood icon to Australia. This vision inspired the theme for the November event: Carnevale Meets Hollywood Masquerade Ball. The February launch became an opportunity to lay the groundwork for this grand affair while showcasing the magic and elegance of Venetian Carnevale to captivate Melbourne and beyond.

Bringing a Hollywood star to Australia, however, meant I needed the right connections. The 'Event Negotiator' mentioned having a trusted contact in the U.S. who had successfully secured talent for Australian events in the past. This contact, she assured me, could bridge the gap and help me achieve the vision I had for the November gala. A connection was made, and for the first time in months, I felt a glimmer of hope. Perhaps this was the missing piece—the catalyst that could tie everything together and ensure the November gala would stand out as the crowning moment of Carnevale Australia.

Once the connection was established, the fee agreed upon, and the contract signed, one of my requests was that I meet the actor during my upcoming trip in August 2017. This trip came about through a so-called friend—a reality TV star whom I had supported tirelessly during her ordeals with the show, often at all hours of the night. She had been invited to the U.S. for a charity event in New York and casually asked if I'd like to accompany her, naturally at my own expense.

After discussing it with my husband, I decided it was an opportunity to kill two birds with one stone. The trip would allow me to make crucial connections while fulfilling her request. We planned to stop in Los Angeles, where she had business to attend to, and I would seize the opportunity to meet the talent broker who had arranged the connection with the Hollywood star. From there, we would travel to New York for her charity event. On the way back, I planned to finalise arrangements with the actor for Carnevale by meeting them in person, once the broker facilitated the introduction.

With the vision of Carnevale Australia beginning to take shape, February 11, 2017, marked the first major milestone: the Masquerade Ball, an evening designed to set the tone for the two-week festival later in the year. The venue was booked not only for this event but also for the grand November gala, ensuring a seamless connection between the two. The February event was all about creating an atmosphere of elegance, fun, and theatricality—a preview of the magic that would follow.

The talent lineup for the evening was nothing short of extraordinary. I wanted to ensure the entertainment captured the glamour and excitement of the Venetian tradition while appealing to a broad audience. We featured a Madonna lookalike whose performance was so convincing she sounded like the real thing, a Kylie Minogue tribute act endorsed by Kylie herself, and an Elvis impersonator who looked and sounded uncannily like The King. Each act brought their own flair to the event, ensuring guests were thoroughly entertained.

The guests didn't hold back either. Many went to great lengths to embrace the Carnevale spirit, creating or hiring elaborate costumes that rivalled anything seen in Venice. Some even had matching ensembles custom-made for the occasion, and their creativity and dedication were rewarded with prizes for the best dressed. The energy and excitement in the room were palpable—it was clear that everyone had come ready to revel in the Carnevale experience.

The evening began with a VIP pre-dinner function that truly set the tone for the night. Guests were treated to champagne and the freshest seafood, complemented by exquisite canapés, all while being serenaded by a talented tenor. The soft notes of his performance added an air of sophistication and romance, creating an intimate and luxurious atmosphere before the main event.

The main ballroom was a feast for the senses. Decorated with Venetian-themed backdrops, the space transported guests straight to the grandeur of Venice. Every detail, from the lighting to the table settings, was carefully curated to immerse attendees in the magic of Carnevale. It was a night of glamour, joy, and escapism—a perfect reflection of the Venetian tradition that inspired it.

The evening was so jam-packed with entertainment and activities that there wasn't a moment for guests to be bored. In fact, some attendees later joked—or half-complained—that they didn't even go to the restroom, fearing they might miss something. It was a testament to the energy of the evening and the seamless flow of performances, which kept everyone fully engaged from start to finish.

The accolades and glowing reviews that poured in after the evening were nothing short of amazing. Guests were effusive in their praise, and the success of the event had already translated into secured bookings for the November gala. While I wasn't entirely surprised—my events had consistently received positive feedback in the past—there was still a lingering sense of nervousness. Beneath the outward success, I was battling internal turmoil that left me on edge.

The amount of money I was stealing from my client to feed my gambling addiction and finance these events was becoming alarmingly larger. Every glowing review seemed to magnify the guilt I carried. Each time I took more, I felt a desperate mixture of justification and shame—a futile attempt to stay afloat in the chaos I had created. Sometimes, I found myself questioning why I had given up my successful bookkeeping and administration business for this. That career had been stable, predictable, and respectable. Yet, there was no denying the thrill I felt when bringing events to life—the creative energy, the connections, the sense of accomplishment. Unfortunately, with that excitement came a darker side: I seemed to attract leeches, people who drained my resources and tested my resolve at every turn.

The two-week festival was shaping up to be an extraordinary cultural celebration, bringing the rich heritage of Venice to Melbourne. Inspired by Carnevale's 800-year-old traditions, the festival was envisioned as a vibrant blend of Italy's artistic, culinary, and cultural legacy, offering Melburnians a unique opportunity to immerse themselves in a sensory journey unlike any other.

The festival's highlight would be the grand Hollywood Meets Carnevale Masquerade Ball, a glittering event that promised to combine the allure of Hollywood with the magic of a Venetian Grand Ball. Adding to its star-studded appeal, I had secured the attendance of Hollywood legend Jane Seymour, whose elegance and charm would elevate the evening. Jane's participation extended beyond this spectacular night—she would also feature in a more intimate theatre event, Up Close & Personal with Jane Seymour, sharing insights into her illustrious career and philanthropic work. These two events would serve as the pinnacle of the festival, bringing together glamour, sophistication, and meaningful engagement.

The festival wasn't just about its headline events; it was an ambitious undertaking designed to celebrate the richness of Italian culture and bring people together in a meaningful way. Beyond the grandeur of the Hollywood Meets Carnevale Masquerade Ball, I envisioned a two-week journey that would immerse attendees in Italy's culinary, artistic, and cultural heritage.

Planning these events was both exhilarating and daunting. Each idea felt like an opportunity to connect with a different audience, and I poured myself into creating a diverse program that would leave no one untouched by the magic of Italian traditions. Among the highlights were concepts that truly brought Italy to Melbourne, including a Gin & Vodka Festival, which offered artisan tastings and demonstrations; a Champagne and Prosecco Festival, a sparkling toast to Italy's finest wines; and a Pizza & Beer Festival, combining comfort food with gourmet flair.

The fashion shows were another passion project, blending the timeless elegance of Italian designers with the creative energy of Melbourne's local talent. It was a celebration of style, history, and innovation—an embodiment of the cultural bridge I hoped this festival would build.

These events would not only highlight Italy's culinary and artistic richness but also create engaging experiences for all ages. Community engagement lay at the heart of the festival's vision. From interactive children's workshops and face painting to live storytelling and music, every detail was designed to foster a warm, inclusive atmosphere. The festival would also feature live theatre productions and screenings of classic Italian films, offering attendees an opportunity to delve deeper into Italy's cinematic and cultural history.

The scope of the festival was ambitious, but I was determined to make it a reality. Securing Jane Seymour for the signature events had been a pivotal step, facilitated through a U.S. talent broker introduced by the 'Event Negotiator' whom we will call Ana. Once the contract was signed, I made it a point to include a personal meeting with Jane during my August trip to the U.S. This trip, a mix of opportunity and serendipity, would allow me to finalise key details while forging stronger connections for the festival's success.

The two-week festival wasn't just about showcasing Italian culture—it was a way to bring people together and create lasting memories. Looking to the months ahead, I was filled with both excitement and trepidation. Every event planned, every detail considered, was a step toward not only delivering an extraordinary festival but also proving to myself that I could overcome the challenges that had once seemed insurmountable.

Chapter 13

A Trip of Mixed Realities

By the end of May, the pieces for my U.S. trip were falling into place. The journey was a carefully orchestrated blend of professional obligations and personal detours, aimed at finalising arrangements for *Carnevale Australia*, meeting Jane Seymour, and exploring new connections to elevate the festival's profile. Accompanying me was Prue, a reality TV celebrity I had supported tirelessly through her tumultuous rise to fame. When she invited me to join her at a charity event in the Hamptons, it seemed like a perfect opportunity to align her plans with mine.

Though she insisted I cover all bookings with promises of reimbursement, my limited credit worked to my advantage—I couldn't afford two business-class airfares. As a result, she purchased her own ticket, but I still covered accommodations for both of us in Los Angeles, New York, and the Hamptons.

With the festival's vision beginning to take shape, I left Ana, the self-proclaimed 'Event Negotiator,' in charge of key logistics for the week-long festival preceding the Masquerade Ball. Ana's relentless assurances about her vast network and ability to sell thousands of tickets had convinced me to entrust her with tasks like gathering infrastructure quotes and drafting a budget. However, I remained heavily involved in shaping the creative direction and ensuring the festival aligned with my standards.

The journey to Los Angeles started smoothly. I met with the broker who had facilitated Jane Seymour's participation, and he turned out to be an absolute delight—professional, warm, and accommodating. He reassured me that on my return trip, he would arrange a personal meeting with Jane to finalise plans for the festival. His confidence was a relief, and I left the meeting feeling optimistic.

From Los Angeles, Prue and I travelled to New York in preparation for the charity event in the Hamptons. Upon checking into our hotel, the owner recognised Prue from her Australian reality show and upgraded us to the top floor. Although I had paid for the accommodation, Prue immediately claimed the larger bedroom with the ensuite, leaving me with a cramped space barely fitting my suitcase. She made sure to remind me that the upgrade was due to her fame—a jab I chose to ignore, focusing instead on the professional opportunities ahead.

Spending more time with Prue, however, began to expose cracks in our friendship. Prue's self-centred behaviour became harder to ignore. One evening, she insisted we visit a trendy bar but demanded I book the reservation under her name. When I used mine instead, it sparked an argument that revealed the growing cracks in our friendship. Her obsession with status overshadowed what should have been a simple outing. She was furious, insisting that booking it under her name would guarantee us the best table. I reminded her that I was her friend, not her personal assistant, and if she wanted to use her name, she could have made the call herself. She accused me of not respecting her, to which I calmly replied that I respected her as a friend—not as a reality TV star.

Despite the tension, we went to the bar. It was an underground venue, charming but not extraordinary. Our table seemed perfectly fine to me, but Prue continued to fixate on the supposed missed opportunity of booking under her name. On our way out, I struck up a conversation with a man I assumed was security, sharing my honest thoughts about the venue. He surprised me by revealing that he was the owner and appreciated my feedback. I introduced him to Prue, who dismissed him as 'just security' once we left, insisting the real owner wouldn't stand at the door. Her snobbery was both irritating and disheartening, but I chose to let it go.

The trip was becoming an eye-opener. While I was achieving my professional goals, my personal dynamic with Prue was unravelling. Her constant need for validation and superiority was exhausting. Yet, I reminded myself that this trip was bigger than her—it was about making Carnevale Australia a reality and ensuring its success.

Back home, Ana's contributions—or lack thereof—were proving to be another source of frustration. She continued to insist that she had unparalleled experience, yet her inability to complete even the most basic tasks cast serious doubt on her claims. I had asked her to draft an event plan, a critical requirement for the venue contract. Weeks passed with nothing but excuses, so I finally handed her a previous event plan I had prepared as a template. Instead of using it as a guide, she dismissed it as something she called by 'a different name,' though she never clarified what that name was. It became evident that I would have to remain deeply involved to ensure the festival's success.

Despite these challenges, my determination remained steadfast. The stakes were high, the financial strain immense, and the pressure relentless, but *Carnevale Australia* wasn't just another event—it was a chance to rebuild, create something extraordinary, and prove to myself that I could rise above the chaos.

Throughout the trip, I was bombarded with calls from Ana at all hours of the night. Her constant interruptions left me sleep-deprived, but I felt compelled to take every call to ensure that everything was running smoothly back home. The stakes were too high to risk jeopardising the events. Each time we spoke, I pressed her for updates on the quotes, the event plan, and ticket sales. She consistently assured me that things were progressing well—there was significant interest from exhibitors, and she claimed ticket sales would be a breeze.

I had Ana liaising with my trusted web designer, AV supplier, and graphic designer, but the feedback I received from them painted a different picture. She continually requested changes to the web designs, creating unnecessary delays, and was extremely demanding with the graphic designer, often blaming them for issues that stemmed from her unclear direction. The AV supplier, growing increasingly frustrated, emailed me to express his concerns. He explained that pinning Ana down for a site inspection at the venue—a critical step for providing an accurate quote—was proving almost impossible.

When I confronted Ana about these issues, she always had reasonable answers that seemed to make sense in the moment, and I reluctantly accepted them. I told myself that hiccups were to be expected in such a large-scale project, but her pattern of deflection and disorganisation was starting to raise red flags.

Between Ana's calls and Prue's frequent tantrums, I found myself with very little peace. I was being pulled in every direction, juggling professional responsibilities and personal challenges. The lack of sleep and constant stress were taking their toll, but I kept pushing forward, clinging to the hope that everything would eventually come together.

It was time to leave New York and head to the Hamptons, where I had booked a charming bed-and-breakfast with two bedrooms—one for Prue and one for myself. When we arrived, the house was breathtaking, a quintessential Hamptons home with its airy elegance and picturesque surroundings. As we explored the rooms, it was clear one was larger than the other. This time, I firmly told Prue that the larger bedroom would be mine since she had claimed the bigger room during our stay in New York. She wasn't pleased, but to my relief, she accepted it without too much fuss.

It quickly became apparent how incompetent Prue was at basic life skills— she couldn't even boil an egg. The next morning, she asked me to make her breakfast, a request that struck me as absurd. I told her flatly that I wasn't her housekeeper. Undeterred, she continued to pester me, so to keep the peace, I grudgingly agreed to make her an egg-white omelette—but only if she washed the dishes. The look on her face was priceless, a mixture of shock and indignation, but hunger won out, and she reluctantly agreed. It was a small victory for me.

The charity luncheon that afternoon was hosted in a stunning beachfront home, its serene waves and golden sand creating a picture-perfect backdrop. Yet, the beauty of the setting couldn't mask the event's shortcomings, from limited food options to an underwhelming sense of hospitality. The guest list was full of reality TV stars, none of whom I recognised, though Prue seemed to know them all. She was in her element, flitting from one group to another, posing for photos and basking in the attention. Meanwhile, I found myself largely on my own. Not once did she introduce me to the hostess or anyone else. I felt like a mere accessory, dragged along to serve as her handbag for the day.

The event itself, despite its glamour, was underwhelming in terms of hospitality. Tickets ranged from USD $5,000 for gold, USD $2,500 for silver, and USD $1,000 for general admission, yet there was shockingly little food. Alcohol flowed freely, but the lack of sustenance left me starving. Knowing my low tolerance for alcohol, I stuck to water, determined to maintain my composure. As the hours dragged on, I couldn't help but wonder how such a high-priced event could fail so spectacularly in meeting basic expectations.

When we finally left, Prue announced that we were attending another function that evening. Two other people would pick us up, and she promised it would be an amazing party hosted by a top-notch brand. I hoped for the best—surely, this event would make up for the disappointments of the day.

The evening party was set on the beach, under a beautiful marquee. While the setup was undeniably impressive, the issues from earlier repeated themselves. Once again, there was very little food, and to make matters worse, the temperature had dropped, leaving us all shivering. We didn't stay long; hunger and cold drove us to leave in search of warmth and sustenance. To our dismay, we discovered that most places were closed at that late hour, leaving us no choice but to go to bed hungry.

Back in New York for a couple more days before heading to Los Angeles, Prue mentioned she had been invited to a function on our last night with the two gentlemen we had met in the Hamptons. Not once did she ask if I would like to join them or even acknowledge what I might do with myself that evening. It was as though my presence was an afterthought. I found it inconsiderate but chose to focus on enjoying my own plans instead.

I decided to explore Eataly, a culinary destination I had always wanted to visit. It turned out to be a delightful escape. I treated myself to a beautiful plate of pasta paired with a glass of red wine, savouring the flavours and the lively ambiance of the place. After dinner, I wandered through the illuminated streets of New York, soaking in the energy of the city and revelling in the freedom of being on my own. By the time I returned to the hotel, it was around 10:30 p.m.

To my surprise, Prue and the two gentlemen were in the hotel lobby. The men greeted me warmly but seemed surprised to see me. They apologised for not including me in their plans, explaining that they had assumed I already had other arrangements. Prue, however, stood silently, making no effort to address the situation. I reassured them that it was fine, sharing how much I had enjoyed my solo evening exploring New York. I mentioned the incredible pasta I had for dinner, which drew envious remarks—they admitted that the function they attended had no food, and by the time they returned to the hotel, the kitchen had closed.

While I didn't vocalise it, a small part of me felt a twinge of satisfaction that Prue had missed out on a proper meal after her dismissiveness. Her behaviour throughout the trip had been self-centred and increasingly grating. This was just another example of her disregard, and it reaffirmed what I had been coming to realise: our friendship was far more one-sided than I had ever imagined.

Back in Los Angeles, we stayed at another B&B, this time with the house entirely to ourselves. However, the property turned out to be nothing like the photos in the listing. It felt strange and underwhelming, but I was determined to make the best of it. Prue, as always, managed to make things about her, though she did have a friend in LA whom we spent quite a bit of time with. He was lovely—kind, accommodating, and refreshingly grounded. Yet, Prue's demanding nature overshadowed much of the time we spent with him. She expected us to cater to her every whim, and navigating her moods felt like a constant balancing act.

Amidst this dynamic, my broker came through with fantastic news: I would finally get to meet Jane Seymour at her Malibu home. This was a crucial step in solidifying her participation in Carnevale Australia, and I couldn't have been more excited. However, Malibu was miles away from where we were staying, so I arranged for a car to take me there and another to bring me back.

When I told Prue about the meeting, she immediately announced that she wanted to come along. I hesitated. This was a business meeting—a pivotal one—and I didn't need anyone else there, especially not someone who had a tendency to make everything about herself. I knew her presence would likely derail the discussion and shift the focus. I explained this to her, pointing out that just as I hadn't intruded on her New York function, she should respect that this was a professional engagement for me.

Naturally, this led to arguments. Prue couldn't see past her desire to be included and seemed offended that I wouldn't acquiesce. It wasn't until her LA friend stepped in that things shifted. While out with her, he gently persuaded her to let it go, emphasising the importance of boundaries in professional matters. When she returned from their outing, she told me that, after thinking it over, she had decided I was right—it wasn't appropriate for her to attend the meeting. What she didn't know was that her friend had already called me to explain how much effort it had taken to convince her.

Ultimately, I was grateful to have avoided what could have been a disruptive presence at such an important meeting. That moment crystallised a realisation that had been building throughout the trip: Prue's relentless need for attention was incompatible with the focus and space I required to pursue my goals. Still, I chose to focus on the positive—this meeting with Jane was a critical milestone for Carnevale Australia, and I was determined to make it count.

The next day, Jane herself called to confirm the time for our meeting. She invited me for morning tea at her Malibu home, and I couldn't help but feel a mix of excitement and nerves. This was a Hollywood icon I had admired for years, and hosting her in Melbourne for Carnevale Australia felt like a dream within reach.

When I arrived at her home, perched above the stunning Malibu coastline, Jane greeted me with such warmth and kindness that it felt as though we had known each other for years. Despite her celebrity status, she was incredibly down-to-earth, warm, and welcoming, instantly making me feel at ease. Her graciousness and genuine interest in both the festival and in me as a person were humbling. It was clear that her elegance extended far beyond her public persona—she truly radiated authenticity.

Her home was quintessentially Malibu, with breathtaking views of the ocean that seemed to stretch endlessly. As we sat down for tea with her partner, David, our conversation flowed effortlessly. Jane's natural curiosity and her enthusiasm for the festival's purpose left me feeling inspired and validated. She shared stories from her illustrious career, as well as her philanthropic endeavours, which deepened my admiration for her.

During the visit, I also had the pleasure of meeting her talented musician son, Chris, who stopped by briefly. Like his mother, he was warm and humble, adding to the genuine and grounded atmosphere of the entire experience.

Before I knew it, the hours had slipped away, and it was time to leave. Before parting, we took some photos together, capturing the memory of what had been an incredible experience. As I drove away, my excitement for hosting Jane in Melbourne later that year only grew stronger. Meeting her had been everything I hoped for and more—her down-to-earth demeanour, warmth, and enthusiasm would undoubtedly elevate the festival to new heights. Her sincerity and encouragement left me more determined than ever to make the event unforgettable.

When I returned to the house, Prue bombarded me with a million questions about my meeting with Jane, which I willingly answered. She listened intently, nodding as I shared the details of the experience. Surprisingly, she took kudos for having made the 'right decision' in not attending, saying it was clearly my moment and my event. While I appreciated her acknowledgment, I also knew that her decision had been strongly influenced by her friend's persuasion. Still, I let it go, not wanting to dampen the mood.

It was our last night in Los Angeles, and Prue's friend had arranged something special—a dinner at Catch, one of LA's top Hollywood hotspots. The kind of place where tables are impossible to get unless you're someone important or have booked months in advance. Thankfully, her friend had the right connections and managed to secure us a table at short notice.

The buzz of the evening was palpable as we arrived at the renowned rooftop restaurant. The ambiance was electric, with stunning views of the city that immediately captivated me. I was so mesmerised by the lights and the skyline that I found myself glued to my phone, snapping photos to capture the moment.

In my awe, I ended up missing a few key Hollywood sightings. At one point, Prue leaned over and whispered excitedly, 'Wesley Snipes just walked by!' But by the time I turned around, he was gone. I couldn't help but laugh at myself for being too engrossed in the view to notice. The evening felt like the perfect way to end the trip—a taste of Hollywood glamour, delicious food, and the kind of buzz that made LA unforgettable.

The dinner was nothing short of spectacular—delicious, fresh seafood that melted in your mouth, perfectly paired with the vibrant ambiance of Catch. It was the kind of meal you wanted to linger over, savouring every bite. When the bill arrived, I paid my portion, feeling satisfied with how the evening had unfolded so far.

But, as had become an unfortunate pattern, Prue found a way to dampen the mood. She launched into a tirade, questioning why I wasn't leveraging people like Kim Kardashian for the festival, claiming Kim would sell it out in no time. I calmly explained that while Kim is undoubtedly influential, she wasn't relevant to the ethos of my events. The demographics for the festival simply wouldn't align with her audience. My focus has always been on authenticity, connection, and creating meaningful experiences—values that transcend the allure of celebrity appeal.

The conversation quickly became heated. Prue wouldn't let it go, insisting that I was missing out on an obvious opportunity. I felt my frustration boil over. I did warn her that if she didn't stop, I would be leaving. But Prue continued, dismissing my perspective entirely.

I'd had enough. Without another word, I stood up, walked downstairs, and ordered an Uber to take me back to the house. Sitting in the car, my anger simmered. What should have been a glamorous evening capped off by good food and great views had instead been marred by yet another clash with Prue.

As the city lights blurred past the car window, I resolved not to let her negativity ruin what was otherwise a successful and productive trip. The festival was my focus, and I wouldn't let anyone derail the vision I had worked so hard to create.

Back at the house, my phone wouldn't stop ringing—it was Prue and her friend. I ignored every call, unwilling to engage after the evening's drama. The emotional drain of dealing with her had left me utterly exhausted. All I wanted was a few hours of peace before our early flight back home.

I climbed into bed, determined to get some much-needed sleep. As I lay there, I made a promise to myself: Once back in Melbourne, I would finalise the accounts, send her the details, and cut ties for good. Prue was toxic—she used and abused people, discarding them the moment they no longer served her purpose. I had seen her do it to others, and now, it was my turn.

Looking back, I couldn't believe how much I had overlooked during the few years I had known her. She had never paid for a single ticket to any of my events, despite attending more than a few. And those so-called 'friends' she boasted about? Not one had bought a ticket, either. She had contributed nothing but empty promises and endless drama.

I had always held onto the belief that people could change, that second chances were worth giving. But this trip marked the breaking point. Prue had revealed her true self in ways I could no longer ignore or excuse.

The next morning, Prue acted as though nothing had happened. I couldn't wait to leave LA and return to Melbourne, ready to immerse myself in the festival preparations. The trip had been draining, but it reaffirmed my priorities. Carnevale Australia was my focus, and I was determined to make it a success, leaving behind the drama and toxicity of those who didn't belong in my journey.

Chapter 14

Unmasking the Chaos

Returning to Melbourne, I was met with a mix of relief and apprehension. The U.S. trip had been an emotional rollercoaster, filled with moments of inspiration and significant challenges. Visiting Jane Seymour at her Malibu home rekindled my passion for Carnevale Australia, but the lingering issues with Prue and Ana left me feeling emotionally drained. Eager to immerse myself in festival preparations, I was unaware of the storm brewing beneath the surface.

A few weeks after my return, Prue called, questioning my silence. I explained that I was busy trying to salvage the event. During my U.S. trip, most of what I heard from her revolved around her broken relationship—spying on her partner to uncover hidden funds and portraying him as controlling. The constant drama had taken a toll, leaving me emotionally spent even before dealing with the chaos Ana had caused back home.

Prue often insisted she wasn't a gold digger, but her fixation on money painted a different picture. Her partner had raised her children from a previous relationship and funded their education at one of Melbourne's best private schools. Yet, she seemed determined to portray him negatively. At one point, she even asked me to provide an affidavit about their relationship. I refused, explaining that I barely knew him. This decision frustrated her, adding another layer to my emotional strain.

Troubles with Ana surfaced soon after my return to Melbourne. Long-time collaborators—my web designer, graphic designer, and AV supplier—expressed frustration with her abrasive attitude, erratic demands, and blame-shifting. These were trusted professionals I had worked with for years, and their growing discontent was deeply concerning.

From the very beginning, Ana had confidently assured me that the festival space would be far too small, citing her expectations of massive crowds. She even requested detailed site plans and dimensions, claiming she needed to calculate the available square meters to 'ensure everything would fit.' At first, her claims seemed credible, but as planning progressed, cracks began to show.

Her projections were not only overly optimistic but increasingly detached from reality.

Adding to the chaos, Ana failed to provide a complete budget or quotes for festival infrastructure despite my repeated requests. Instead, she dismissed my concerns with vague reassurances that ticket sales and exhibitor fees would more than cover costs. Her overly optimistic outlook left me with a nagging sense of dread. Yet, I held onto hope, determined to see the event through despite the mounting challenges.

Ultimately, when the challenges became insurmountable, I was forced to make the heartbreaking decision to cancel the event. Ana's true colours emerged at this point. Rather than acknowledging her role in the missteps, she flatly denied her earlier claims and deflected all blame onto me. It became painfully clear that Ana had a pattern of avoiding accountability—it was always someone else's fault. This realisation was both frustrating and disheartening, leaving me to shoulder the consequences of her misguided assurances.

The breaking point came with my PR company. While I was away, Ana had been given full access to them—a decision I now deeply regret. Upon my return, I discovered that my PR consultant was liaising through Ana instead of directly with me. Attempts to address the situation only made things worse, as my PR consultant sided with Ana. Feeling betrayed, I had no choice but to let the PR company go—less than a month before Jane's arrival in Australia. Scrambling for a replacement, I managed to secure one, though at a much higher cost due to the tight timeline.

As part of Jane's visit, I also wanted to host a private dinner for 20 people at one of Melbourne's top restaurants. The event had a specific budget, and I carefully curated the guest list to include key supporters of my events. I also allowed Ana to invite a few of her contacts as a gesture of gratitude for their contributions. One of her guests, a jeweller, generously offered to gift each attendee a small diamond as a token of appreciation—a thoughtful touch that added an extra layer of elegance to the evening.

On the day of the dinner, I sent Ana a detailed running sheet outlining the evening's schedule, which included me welcoming the guests and expressing my gratitude. However, unbeknownst to me, Ana had assumed she would take on the role of hostess, deliver the speech, and lead the event. When I clarified that this wasn't her role—especially as I was covering all the expenses—she was visibly displeased. I stood firm, insisting that I would lead the evening as planned.

Despite the initial tension, the dinner proceeded smoothly—until the very end. Towards the conclusion of the evening, Ana took it upon herself to collect the diamonds gifted to my husband and son, without their consent. When we arrived home and I learned what had happened, I was furious, but let it go.

To make matters worse, I later discovered that after Jane, my family and I had left the venue, Ana had ordered an additional bottle of French champagne for herself and her partner, which was added to my account without my knowledge. Her blatant disregard for boundaries and respect left me feeling betrayed and deeply frustrated.

Ana had also taken over communication with Jane Seymour's team after convincing me it was logical since she had introduced me to the contact. This led to complications. Ana suggested extending Jane's stay in Australia, offering her visits to iconic destinations like Uluru. Jane was thrilled at the idea, but I made it clear my company couldn't fund such an extensive itinerary. Ana assured me she would secure sponsorships, but weeks passed, and her promises proved empty.

With time running out, I had no choice but to take control. Leveraging my personal network, I arranged a five-day stay for Jane and her partner at Qualia, a secluded resort on Hamilton Island. It was a bespoke experience, including a private excursion to the Great Barrier Reef and exclusive use of a motor yacht to explore the Whitsundays. Building on this success, I secured a four-day stay at The Darling in Sydney, complete with a penthouse, a harbour cruise, and a chauffeured tour of the city. While Ana only managed to organise a complimentary Harbour Bridge climb, most of the arrangements had fallen on my shoulders.

The Melbourne Cup brought yet another saga. Jane's assistant had asked Ana in advance about the dress code, and I was surprised to hear from Jane that Ana had told her assistant it was a black and white affair. I wasn't made aware of this until Jane arrived in Melbourne, and we were in her penthouse. Jane expressed her confusion, mentioning she thought the Melbourne Cup was supposed to be colourful. I confirmed that she was right—vibrant attire is traditional for the event. A local fashion designer had created a black-and-white outfit for her based on Ana's instructions. In a last-minute effort to add some colour, Jane paired the outfit with her own black-and-red cape. While she carried it off beautifully, the situation was embarrassing and entirely avoidable.

Despite the setbacks, I poured my energy into the Carnevale Ball and Jane Seymour's events, determined to salvage my vision. These events became a testament to resilience and the power of turning challenges into triumphs. Moving forward, I vowed to trust my instincts, value lasting relationships, and never again place blind faith in someone who hadn't earned it.

As I have mentioned before, I always incorporate a charity into my events, and this Carnevale was no different. Knowing that Jane was a close friend of Olivia Newton-John, I naturally assumed Olivia's charity would be the one we would support. However, Ana informed me that Jane had chosen The Next Step Spinal Cord Injury Recovery Centre, run by Rhiannon Tracey. I found it odd, but since Ana assured me this was Jane's choice, I went along with it. I later discovered that Jane had not chosen The Next Step charity, and Ana told Jane that was the charity I had chosen. Ana had made this decision without any consultation with me or Jane. Having made a commitment, I decided to honour our deal, even after learning the truth.

The Carnevale Ball was a resounding success, with guests showering praise not only on the event itself but also on Jane and her partner. The evening began with an exclusive private VIP function, setting the tone for an unforgettable night. Guests were treated to a lavish seafood station adorned with intricately designed ice sculptures, adding a touch of grandeur and sophistication. The attention to detail was extraordinary, creating a sense of luxury that left everyone in awe.

Following the VIP reception, the celebration moved to the main ballroom, where the atmosphere shifted into a dazzling display of entertainment and elegance. The theme for the night was a journey through the golden era of Hollywood to the late '80s, and every detail reflected this nostalgic and glamorous vision. Guests were captivated by performances that brought iconic moments from Hollywood's golden years to life. A Marilyn Monroe impersonator dazzled the audience with her charm and charisma, while tap dancers showcased their electrifying moves, evoking memories of classic musicals. The entertainment seamlessly transitioned through decades, culminating in high-energy performances that celebrated the late '80s with flair.

Jane, ever the gracious guest of honour, ensured that every attendee felt special. She took the time to pose for photos with each guest, creating cherished memories that many would treasure for years to come. Her warm demeanour and genuine interest in the attendees left a lasting impression, adding an extra layer of magic to the evening. Her partner was equally engaging, charming guests with his approachable and friendly manner.

The venue itself was a masterpiece, adorned with elegant Venetian masks, opulent centrepieces, and lighting that transformed the space into a dreamlike setting. The live entertainment, coupled with the vibrant atmosphere, kept the energy high throughout the night, with guests fully immersed in the Carnevale spirit.

As part of the evening, we held a series of auctions that added a meaningful charitable component to the Carnevale Ball. Jane generously donated two of her exquisite *Open Heart* sculptures, which became the centrepiece of the auction and captivated the attendees with their beauty and significance. The bidding was lively and enthusiastic, reflecting the generosity of the guests and their support for the cause.

Thanks to these incredible donations and the overwhelming participation of the attendees, we were able to raise over $18,000 for the charity. The funds were gratefully accepted by Rhiannon, who expressed heartfelt gratitude on behalf of the organisation. She emphasised how much these much-needed contributions would help further their vital work. The room was filled with a sense of shared purpose and accomplishment, adding a deeper layer of meaning to an already unforgettable evening.

The feedback was overwhelmingly positive, with many attendees praising the seamless organisation, breathtaking decor, and extraordinary entertainment. It was clear that the Carnevale Ball had struck the perfect balance between elegance and celebration, offering an experience that would be remembered for years to come. By the end of the evening, it was evident that this event had set a new benchmark for excellence, leaving everyone eagerly anticipating the next grand affair.

After the event, I travelled with Jane and her partner to Sydney and New Zealand for the next two weeks, enjoying a wonderful time in their company. Despite the joy of that trip, I knew deep down that once I returned, I needed to cut ties with Ana. I had endured enough of her broken promises and manipulative behaviour, and I couldn't bear another disastrous relationship. I started to question whether the issue was me—was I too trusting, too willing to believe in others? In some ways, the answer was yes. My trust in people had been my undoing, but this time, I was determined to take control and set boundaries.

However, Ana wasn't someone I could easily forget. Not long after returning, I received a message from someone asking if I was the person who had brought Susan Sarandon, Goldie Hawn, and Jane Seymour to Australia. I confirmed that I was and inquired why they were asking. The response shocked me: Ana had contacted them, presenting herself as 'The Event Negotiator,' claiming that she was the one responsible for bringing these high-profile guests to Australia. Furthermore, she added in her message to the person that she was with Kate Hudson that day, and it would be epic.

Kate Hudson, of course, had been brought out by Business Chicks, and thanks to her mother, Goldie Hawn, I had been fortunate enough to have a one-on-one with Kate. Ana, however, had no connection to her and wasn't even on the guest list for a meet and greet with Kate. I know that if she had been with Kate, she would have had photos taken with her. The audacity of her claims left me stunned.

Messages about Ana's fabrications continued to pour in, prompting me to investigate further. I reached out to several contacts who had worked with Sir Richard Branson and Tim Ferriss in Australia, both of whom Ana claimed to have brought out. Unsurprisingly, I discovered the truth: Ana's role had been limited to selling tickets for their events. Her lack of photos with any of these figures now made sense—she had no real association with them beyond her exaggerated claims.

Then, I checked her website and was appalled. There they were—my photos of my high-profile guests, presented as her own work. I had been extremely generous, including her in group photos at each event, yet she now claimed these events were hers. What's more, in many of the photos, the media walls clearly displayed the event branding and partnerships, contradicting her claims outright. She even advertised these falsehoods on the Business Chicks website, taking credit for these events. Furious, I contacted my lawyer and demanded that she remove the photos and stop misrepresenting them as her own work. While she removed some, 21 photos still remain on her website, continuing to falsely credit her as the host. My lawyer eventually advised me to let it go, but the frustration lingered.

To make matters worse, on her Instagram account, I noticed she has photos of Sophia Loren included as part of a collage of flashbacks showcasing some of the best moments and events. She is claiming an association with Sophia, but the truth is glaringly different—I didn't even know Ana back when I worked with Sophia, and she wasn't even there as a guest. This has left me utterly speechless. It was yet another blatant attempt to fabricate credibility by exploiting others' hard work and achievements.

I remember taking Ana to an international chef's birthday celebration, an event I had been attending for several years, where each year I brought a different guest. That year, I chose to take her. She met the chef for all of two minutes, yet soon after, I discovered she was using a photo I took of her and the chef together on her website, along with his logo, claiming him as one of her clients. It was unbelievable. Ana's audacity knew no bounds—turning fleeting moments into fabricated partnerships and leveraging them to further her deceitful narrative.

This entire ordeal taught me a painful yet valuable lesson: trusting people too easily can come at a high cost. But it also strengthened my resolve to be more discerning and protect the integrity of my work and reputation moving forward.

Despite the turmoil surrounding Ana and the growing chaos in my personal and professional life, I found myself sinking deeper into my own destructive patterns. The betrayal and manipulation I experienced with her only added to the darkness already consuming me. I was still stealing, still gambling, and my depression knew no bounds. The weight of shame and guilt was unbearable, yet I couldn't break free from the cycle I had created.

The events with Ana should have been a wake-up call, a chance to reclaim control over my life, but instead, they pushed me further into isolation. My world was falling apart, and I was clinging to anything that might offer an escape—even if it only made things worse.

As I closed the door on my involvement with Ana, I was left with the harsh reality that while I had cut her out of my life, I hadn't addressed the deeper issues dragging me down. Trusting her had been a mistake, but the hardest truth was that the person I truly couldn't trust was myself.

This chapter of my life wasn't about resolution—it was about unravelling. And as much as I longed for a way out, I didn't yet know how to find it. Instead, I kept gambling, kept stealing, and kept falling, wondering how much further I could go before I hit rock bottom.

Chapter 15

A Milestone Year

The year 2018 was a turning point in my life—marked by some incredible highs and devastating lows. It began with a milestone: my 60th birthday. For me, birthdays were never an annual event but rather a rare occasion celebrated only once every ten years. This one felt especially significant, not just because of the number, but because I knew it would be my dad's last birthday celebration on this earth.

Determined to make it meaningful, I organised two celebrations. The first was for friends and supporters—a way to honour those who had been part of my journey, through its ups and downs. The second was an intimate gathering with family, a chance to create memories with those closest to me while we still had the time.

At first glance, it seemed like a year that started with so much joy and love, but as the months unfolded, 2018 would challenge me in ways I couldn't have anticipated. My milestone birthday was not just a marker of age but also the beginning of a year that would test my resilience, faith, and ability to find light even in the darkest moments.

The celebration with friends and supporters took place on the rooftop of a Melbourne building owned by some dear friends. The setting was perfect— a vibrant night themed around the 70s and 80s, complete with catering that matched the nostalgic atmosphere. It was a night filled with laughter, music, and dancing, and for a brief moment, I allowed myself to revel in the joy of it all. At least, that's how it felt at the time. In hindsight, it's amazing how people who seem like friends stick around when they perceive you as successful, buzzing around like bees to honey. But when life takes a downturn, those same people are often the first to vanish. It was a bittersweet realisation that lingered after the party ended.

The family celebration, on the other hand, was intimate and deeply personal, held at a cosy family restaurant. This gathering carried a weight of its own. My father, who had always been a pillar of strength and self-assurance, needed the waiters to lift his chair to help him up the stairs. Walking was no longer an option for him. The previous year, he had been diagnosed with progressive supranuclear palsy (PSP), a late-onset neurodegenerative disease that affects specific areas of the brain. The symptoms—loss of balance, slowed movements, difficulty with eye coordination, and cognitive decline—were devastating.

We weren't sure if this condition was related to the brain tumour he had battled a decade earlier, but it was heartbreaking to watch him deteriorate. Seeing such a strong, self-reliant man reduced to needing help with even the simplest tasks—unable to walk, talk, or eat on his own—was profoundly painful. Despite the challenges, we were determined to make this celebration as special as possible, cherishing the time we had left with him.

Five months later, my dad was gone. He passed away in June at the age of 84. While his passing was a blessing for him—freeing him from the pain and limitations of his condition—it was deeply painful for us, his family. The loss left a void that nothing could fill.

My mum was utterly distraught. Their bond had been unshakable, a lifetime of love and companionship that now felt cruelly severed. Her grief was overwhelming, and it placed extra pressure on us siblings to ensure she was never alone. We did everything we could to comfort her, but her longing to be with him was palpable. She would often say, through her tears, that she wished to leave this world and join her beloved husband. Watching her heartbreak compounded our own, as we struggled to navigate the grief of losing not just our father, but a part of her as well.

In February 2018, I attended a function in Sydney with a friend, where we met a woman who seemed to be on her own. She struck up a conversation with us, and we quickly warmed to her, thinking she was solo at the event. It wasn't until later, when her husband returned that we realised she wasn't alone. For the sake of this story, I'll call her Mary. We struck up a friendship, and after returning to Melbourne, we kept in touch.

A few months later, I held a small event in Melbourne—a pizza and beer matching degustation—and Mary and her husband purchased tickets. She seemed pleasant enough, and I introduced her to a few people in Melbourne. During her visit, we ended up in her hotel room, chatting about various things, including her fine hair. I mentioned a contact I had who sold wigs—I had even bought one for my birthday—and we decided to call her. The wig seller came to the hotel, and Mary ordered two wigs while I ordered another one. We both paid upfront. Unfortunately, that woman disappeared shortly after, taking our money and leaving us without the wigs.

Mary shared some troubling stories during that visit—how she had destroyed her brother's political career, her ongoing issues with her mother, and strained relationships with her siblings. Looking back, I realise I should have read the signs, but my desperation to break into the Sydney market with my events clouded my judgment. I clung to the hope that Mary could open doors for me in Sydney.

She asked me to visit Sydney, promising to introduce me to influential people. Of course, the trip was at my expense. I arranged my accommodation at the Star Casino and even booked a room for her and her husband under my name and paid with my casino dollars which I had accumulated during my many visits. For someone who claimed to be a multimillionaire, she was surprisingly tight with money. I ended up paying for their entire weekend.

Mary had a big mouth, and her connections were undeniable—she seemed to know everyone in high-profile positions. But her loose tongue was another story. She freely divulged secrets about her so-called friends, sharing astonishing details about people I would never repeat. Despite her connections, her behaviour left me uneasy. Yet, I found myself caught in the illusion that she could be the key to expanding my business in Sydney.

While chatting with Mary, she mentioned that one of her billionaire friends was struggling with his weight. I casually brought up my Sydney chef, who was returning soon from overseas. He had a remarkable talent for designing personalised menus that promoted health and fitness, and I offered to introduce them. Upon returning to Melbourne, I discussed the idea with my chef, who agreed to meet Mary and see if he could help her friend.

We also talked about planning more events to recover the money we had lost from the Goldie Hawn event. So, on May 8, 2018, I travelled back to Sydney to meet with the chef, discuss potential events, and arrange a dinner to introduce him to Mary. What happened next took me completely by surprise. As we sat down for dinner, it turned out that Mary and the chef had known each other from school and had been searching for each other for years. They were overjoyed to reconnect, and the gratitude they expressed for my introduction made me feel genuinely good. To top it off, the billionaire in question had also gone to school with them, tying their connection even closer. Mary sent me numerous messages afterward, expressing her excitement about the reunion.

I was later invited to return to Sydney for another dinner on May 26, this time to bring everyone together: Mary, her husband, the chef, and the billionaire. They requested a booth at Black, a restaurant that held nostalgic value for them, and I booked it without hesitation. Little did I know, that evening would be one I could never forget—and not in a good way.

When I arrived at the restaurant, I waited for quite some time, receiving strange texts and phone calls from a young woman claiming to be Mary's niece. Her behaviour was erratic and unsettling, but I brushed it off. Eventually, Mary, her husband, the chef, and the niece arrived. The group ordered an extravagant amount of food, wine, and cocktails. While the evening started off awkwardly, I assumed the tension was due to the niece's odd presence.

After dinner, Mary and the chef stepped outside for a cigarette—though she smoked, he didn't—and I was left alone with Mary's husband. What followed was one of the most confronting experiences of my life. Out of nowhere, he produced an invoice for $10,000, claiming it was for the design of Alec Baldwin's menu back in 2016. I was completely blindsided. I had never seen the invoice before, nor had there ever been any discussion about fees. If such fees had been mentioned, I wouldn't have agreed, as I had access to other chefs, including the Crown Casino team, who could have designed the menu without additional cost.

Mary's husband didn't stop there. He accused me of conspiring with a legal firm in Melbourne to steal $100,000 from a trust, a baseless and outrageous claim. The evening escalated further when he demanded that I pay for the dinner—over $2,000—and gave me an ultimatum to settle the invoice within 24 hours or face the consequences. I was stunned and overwhelmed, unable to process what had just happened. Tears welled up in my eyes as I tried to comprehend the betrayal. After they left, I went back to my hotel room and cried my heart out. I didn't sleep that night, consumed by fear and dread about what would happen if I didn't comply.

The next day, a Sunday, I paid the invoice, terrified that my gambling and stealing would be exposed if I didn't. On Monday, I contacted my lawyer and explained what had happened. His immediate response was to tell me not to pay, but it was too late—I had already done so.

Not long after the dinner at Black, I received a letter of demand from Mary's husband. Feeling overwhelmed and uncertain, I forwarded the letter to my lawyer for advice. In the meantime, I finalised the accounting spreadsheet for the partnership. After carefully reviewing all the expenses I had covered, it was clear that there was little I owed the Sydney chef. Despite the evidence, he wasn't happy with the outcome, and tensions continued to escalate.

On Tuesday, June 26, while at my dad's viewing, I received a shocking text message from a business friend in Sydney. Less than 30 minutes earlier, he had received a phone call from a private investigator. The investigator asked if he was aware that I had committed fraud and informed him that they planned to interview him and 312 others before the end of the financial year. My heart sank. The timing couldn't have been more devastating.

The very next morning, on Wednesday, June 27—my dad's funeral day—I started receiving more calls. A couple of business acquaintances reached out, telling me they had also been contacted by a private investigator with similar accusations. What baffled me was how these investigators had obtained their names and numbers. Some of these individuals were mere social media connections, people I barely knew or had interacted with only casually. The reach of this attack felt invasive and relentless, adding another layer of distress to an already unbearable time.

With the situation spiralling out of control, I had no choice but to seek an intervention order against the Sydney chef—not only for myself but also for my husband and son. I had become aware that Mary's husband had shady connections, which only heightened my sense of urgency. The fear of what could happen to my family was overwhelming.

Eventually, the chef agreed to a voluntary undertaking to the court, and I hoped that this would finally put an end to the ordeal. For a brief moment, I allowed myself to believe the matter was resolved, that the harassment would stop, and that I could move forward.

But deep down, I couldn't shake the feeling that this wasn't over. I suspected the chef had gone to the client from whom I had taken the money and revealed my actions. The thought gnawed at me—that this was how my crime was uncovered. It was a bitter realisation, knowing that the chain of events I had set in motion was unravelling everything I had tried to keep hidden.

And then my fears became reality. On September 18, 2018, I took money again, but by the 20th, the funds hadn't been transferred into my account as they always had before. At that moment, I knew—I had been caught. Panic consumed me, and I had no idea what to do. Thoughts of ending my life crept in, a way to escape the shame and the consequences. But then, I thought of my little boy, my husband, and my recently widowed mother. She was 84, and this would destroy her. Still, the weight of the disgrace I had brought upon my family—my boys and my mum—was crushing.

In my desperation, I reached out to a friend, someone who had once been a lawyer but was now retired. For the first time, I confided in someone and told her the whole truth. It was a moment of raw vulnerability, and her response became my lifeline. She listened, guided me, and advised me on what to do next. Sensing the fragile state I was in, she urged me to see my doctor and to be completely honest. I owe her my life—her support and encouragement pulled me back from the edge. Even then, I still couldn't bring myself to tell my husband the truth.

But by September 24, I had no choice. At 8:00 p.m., there was a knock on the door. My son opened it, and I heard a voice ask for me. My heart sank—I knew I was about to be arrested. Bracing myself, I went to the door, but instead of the police, it was someone serving me papers. All he said was, 'Connie Paglianiti, you've been served.' I had heard that phrase in movies countless times, but now it was my reality. Shaking, I took the large envelope and ran to my room.

My husband and son followed, both alarmed. My husband demanded to know what I had been served. Even then, I tried to cover it up, insisting it was nothing to worry about. But they didn't let it go. They pressed harder, and eventually, the dam broke. I confessed everything. The look on their faces was pure shock—a mixture of disbelief and heartbreak.

Then, I heard the softest voice pierce the silence. 'Mother, please don't do anything stupid. I need my mother.' It was my little boy. His words struck me to my core. In that moment, I knew I couldn't end my life, no matter how unbearable things became. I had to face the consequences, and more importantly, I had to stop. No more lies, no more stealing, no more gambling. Gambling had ravaged my life, destroying both my personal and professional worlds.

My husband, shaken, began blaming himself for not noticing the signs, for not realising something was wrong. But I told him the truth: 'I was a damn good actress. I put all my energy into making sure no one knew.' And I had succeeded—until now.

After the papers were served, I informed my lawyer about my situation, and he took over the case. With the weight of everything pressing down on me, I retreated into the confines of my home. I barely went out, except to visit my mum or attend family gatherings. I couldn't bear the thought of them finding out, so I made an effort to keep up appearances.

On social media and through text messages, people began asking if I was okay. Some speculated I had cancer, while others just assumed I was going through a rough time. I told them I wasn't well and needed time away from work, which wasn't far from the truth. The depression was suffocating. My doctor recommended a mental health plan and referred me to a psychologist. She also prescribed antidepressants to help me cope.

On October 1, I faced my initial civil court case at the Supreme Court. It was an overwhelming experience. I arrived with my husband and my lawyer, only to find myself facing at least half a dozen lawyers representing the other side. They came prepared, wielding the power of one of the top five legal firms in the world. Even before the court orders were issued, they had already frozen my accounts. Worse, they froze my son's account as well, simply because he was underage and I was the nominee on the account. It was devastating, knowing the ripple effect of my actions was now impacting him.

My lawyer advised me to apply for bankruptcy. It was a difficult decision, but he explained that it would bring the civil case to an end. Reluctantly, I followed his advice, and the case was dismissed. However, the relief was short-lived. Soon after, they attempted to go after my husband's assets, creating even more strain on our family. The legal battles were relentless, and I couldn't help but feel the enormity of the shame and pain I had brought upon my loved ones.

Although they didn't have any court orders for my husband's accounts, they somehow knew every detail of what went in and out. The level of access they seemed to have was alarming and deeply unsettling. The only way the other side could have known such specific information was if someone inside the bank had provided it to them. When confronted, the bank adamantly denied any wrongdoing, but the coincidence was too glaring to ignore.

The stress of this discovery was overwhelming, especially for my husband. While he considered pursuing the matter further, the emotional and mental toll made it impossible for him to follow through. The strain was already unbearable, and adding another layer of confrontation seemed insurmountable.

In my heart, I believed I knew where this breach originated. Mary's husband had boasted in the past about having contacts in every bank. It wasn't hard to imagine that he had leveraged those connections to access private information and use it against us. The feeling of betrayal and violation was indescribable, as though no aspect of our lives was safe from their reach.

So, on November 1, I was officially declared bankrupt. It was a moment that felt both devastating and inevitable, the culmination of everything that had spiralled out of control in my life. The weight of my actions, the legal battles, and the financial strain had all led to this point. Signing the papers felt like admitting defeat—not just to the system, but to myself.

Bankruptcy brought some relief in that it halted the civil case, but it came with its own set of challenges. The stigma of it hung heavily over me, a constant reminder of the choices I had made and the damage they had caused. It wasn't just about the financial loss—it was about the shame and guilt that now defined my existence. I had lost not only my livelihood but also my sense of identity and self-worth.

The only glimmer of hope was knowing that this could be the bottom, the place where I could finally begin to rebuild. But even that felt distant and uncertain. For now, all I could do was navigate the fallout and try to keep my family afloat, even as the pieces of my life lay shattered around me.

Thousands of dollars later, they finally dropped the case against my husband. While this brought some relief and alleviated part of the burden, it was far from the end of the ordeal. With the civil cases failing, the matter escalated, and I was criminally charged.

In early December 2018, the police came to my door early one morning. When I opened it, I was met with six officers—five men and one woman. They informed me they needed to search the premises. My heart sank as I stepped aside to let them in. I was already overwhelmed with shame, but the thought of them seeing the state of my room added another layer of humiliation.

Over the past few years, my depression had consumed me, and my room reflected the chaos in my mind. Clothes and paperwork were strewn across the bed, the floor, and every piece of furniture. It looked like a bomb had gone off. While the rest of the house was neat and tidy—the public areas maintained for appearances—my room was a stark contrast. It was my private space, a place where I could shut the door and let the mess match the turmoil inside me.

On the outside, I presented myself as neat and organised, but my room told a different story. It was the physical manifestation of how little I cared about my life anymore. Allowing the officers into that space felt like exposing the part of me I had worked so hard to hide—a vulnerable, unfiltered glimpse into the depths of my despair.

The officers seized my laptop, a computer, some bank statements, and my passport before taking me to the police station to give a statement. Although I wanted to plead guilty immediately, my lawyer advised against it. Afterward, they took me to court to appear before a judge. My lawyer couldn't attend as he had another case, but he assured me everything would be fine since the police didn't intend to object to bail.

My husband met me at the court, but I was led to a cell underneath the courtroom while waiting for the proceedings. The cell was horrid—cold, noisy, and disgustingly dirty. It was a place that felt utterly dehumanising, and I sat there for hours, trying to steel myself against the despair creeping in.

Late in the afternoon, I was brought upstairs, where a legal aid lawyer represented me. When the judge set a hefty bond for my release, I thought the nightmare was nearly over. However, since it was so late in the day, there wasn't enough time to finalise the paperwork, and the lawyer made no effort to fight for me. I was sent back downstairs to wait in the same grim cell, now facing the prospect of spending the night there until my husband could return in the morning with the necessary documents.

But at 5:00 p.m., the situation took a drastic turn. An officer called my name and informed me that I was being transferred to Dame Phyllis Frost, a high-security women's prison. Shocked, I tried to explain there must have been a mistake—I was supposed to stay in the holding cell until morning. My arguments fell on deaf ears, and I was ushered into a prisoner transport vehicle. The experience was surreal and humiliating; I felt like a dangerous criminal, shackled and powerless.

As the brawler rattled its way to the prison, I was overwhelmed by claustrophobia and panic attacks. The confined space, combined with the weight of everything that had transpired, made it almost impossible to breathe. My mind raced with fear, guilt, and disbelief that my life had spiralled to this point. By the time we arrived at the prison, I was utterly broken, unsure of how I would face what lay ahead.

As I stepped into the prison, I felt the weight of my actions crash down on me in a way I had never experienced before. The noise, the cold, and the overwhelming sense of fear made it impossible to think clearly. My life, which I had worked so hard to build, was now unrecognisable. Every step felt heavier than the last as I was processed, searched, and assigned a place in this new, harsh reality.

That night, as I lay on the thin, hard mattress in my cell, staring at the cracks in the ceiling, I felt utterly alone. Shame, regret, and fear coursed through me. But alongside them was a tiny flicker of something else—something I couldn't quite name. Was it hope? Resignation? Or just a survival instinct kicking in?

I didn't know it then, but this was the beginning of a new chapter in my life. One where I would have to confront everything I had buried, everything I had avoided, and everything I had done. The road ahead would be brutal, but perhaps it would also hold a chance for redemption.

Chapter 16

A Night That Changed Everything

When I arrived at the jail, the first thing I asked was to make a phone call to my husband. He wasn't aware that I had been transferred from the court to the prison, and I needed to let him know. The officers insisted that he would already be informed, but I knew they were wrong. After much persistence, one officer finally allowed me to make the call. As I suspected, my husband was completely unaware of the transfer. He was shocked and concerned but assured me he would bring all the necessary documentation to the jail the following morning to secure my release.

Next came the strip search—a humiliating experience that I could never have anticipated. I had never been comfortable being naked, not even in front of my husband, and now I was forced to undress in front of a complete stranger. I felt exposed, degraded, and powerless as they inspected me. Afterward, they handed me second-hand clothes that were far too big for me, including underwear I was required to wear. Nothing of my own was allowed.

From there, I was escorted to a cold, stark medical cell, where I was left for hours. The space was vast and freezing, with no sense of humanity or comfort. By the time they came for me, it was close to midnight. They handed me a basket of clothes and made me carry it to another section of the prison. Each step felt heavier than the last as I made my way to what would be my cell for the night.

The cell was stark and unforgiving. A thin mattress lay on a hard metal frame, and a stainless-steel toilet stood in one corner. The walls seemed to close in with every passing moment, amplifying the sense of suffocation. The air was heavy with a mixture of stale confinement and despair, and the floor was filthy, covered in grime that mirrored the hopelessness I felt.

If I thought the holding cell underneath the court was disgusting, this was far worse. The toilet, the floors, and the washbasin were so dirty they made me dry retch. Not that it mattered—I hadn't eaten anything all day or night, so there was nothing to bring up. I refused to drink water, terrified of having to use the toilet, and brushing my teeth in the grimy sink was out of the question.

Instead, I placed the clean blanket they gave me over the bed and lay on top of it, trying to avoid the stained mattress beneath. Tears streamed silently down my face as I stared at the walls, unable to sleep. The noise from the hallways, the harsh fluorescent lights that barely dimmed, and the bone-chilling cold made the night feel endless. My thoughts were relentless—a spiral of shame, regret, and fear. How had I ended up here? How would my family react to all of this?

By morning, I was emotionally and physically drained. When the guards finally came to retrieve me, I felt a flicker of relief that the night was over. But even as I stepped out of that cell, I knew this was far from the end. That single night behind bars, brief as it was, left a mark that I would carry with me forever. It wasn't just a punishment—it was the sharp edge of a truth I could no longer avoid. My life had to change, and this was only the beginning.

My husband provided the relevant papers for the bond, and we were finally able to leave. The ride home was silent—I didn't feel like talking. I was too upset and overwhelmed, uncertain about what the future held. My thoughts were consumed by fear and sadness, making it impossible to focus on anything else.

Shortly after, my lawyer began organising a barrister for my case. When we went to meet her, she delivered devastating news. On a good day, she explained, I was looking at a minimum of six years in prison—possibly up to ten. My heart sank. I couldn't even fathom spending one more night in a cell, let alone years. The thought was unbearable, and I struggled to process what this would mean for me and my family. My mind raced with dark thoughts, but I forced myself to snap out of it. I knew I couldn't give in to despair. My family needed me, and no matter what happened, I had to be strong. I resolved to take whatever punishment was handed to me on the chin, for their sake.

In the meantime, as I waited for a new court date, my retired lawyer friend organised a lunch with a mutual friend. I wasn't comfortable with the idea of socialising, but I also knew I couldn't simply vanish from everyone's lives without explanation. Reluctantly, I agreed to go.

At the lunch, when I shared what had happened, I kept my emotions in check. The antidepressants were working, I wasn't crying at the drop of a hat like before. My lack of visible emotion seemed to unsettle our mutual friend. Later, my lawyer friend told me that the friend had interpreted my composure as a lack of remorse for my crime. Her comment hit me hard. I hadn't intended to come across that way, but it made me question how others might perceive me.

In response, I made a drastic decision—I stopped taking the medication. I wanted to feel something again, to ensure my actions and words didn't appear detached or unfeeling. My doctor wasn't happy with my choice, especially since I had gone cold turkey. She urged me to restart the medication, warning me about the risks of withdrawal. But I couldn't bring myself to do it. The antidepressants had numbed me to the point where I felt like a zombie, disconnected from myself and the gravity of my situation. I didn't want to live that way.

In the meantime, I remained confined to my home, barely venturing out. The isolation was suffocating, but I was fortunate to have a good friend whom I could confide in. She came over one day and helped me clean my room, which had become a chaotic reflection of my mental state. She was an absolute godsend and continues to be a pillar of support in my life. That's what a true friend is—someone who stands by you during the good times and the bad, not just when they can take something from you.

Eventually, I learned that my next court case was scheduled for May 2019. The months leading up to it were filled with anxiety and uncertainty, as I didn't know what to expect. When the day arrived, my husband and I went to court, bracing ourselves for the outcome. However, the police weren't prepared, and a decision couldn't be made. The judge was visibly displeased with their lack of preparation and didn't hold back in expressing his frustration.

While I was relieved that the case was postponed, I couldn't help but feel grateful for the delay. The judge's attitude had been harsh, and I couldn't imagine receiving a fair sentence from him. The postponement gave me a small reprieve, though the weight of what lay ahead remained heavy on my shoulders.

After this court appearance, I started confiding in people I had considered friends. These were people I had supported through their own struggles—

friends I had been there for at all hours, day and night. Some I had even helped financially, including one I saved from eviction by lending them money for rent—a loan they later refused to repay. (But that's another story entirely, and if I were to recount every single thing that happened, I'd be here forever.)

But one comment cut me deeply. Prue, someone I had considered a friend even after our U.S. trip, told a mutual friend, 'Why are you still talking to a criminal?' I was stunned. After everything I had done for her—including paying for all the accommodation and expenses for the U.S. trip, which she never reimbursed—this was how she saw me. That's when it truly hit me: people can be so false. Their support often hinges on what they can gain from you, not genuine care or friendship. I wasn't asking for favours, just some understanding and kindness. But slowly, one by one, these so-called friends began to disappear—not only from my life but also from my social platforms.

One even went as far as advising another mutual friend not to get involved by giving me a reference for court. The betrayal was like a series of small stabs, each one a painful reminder of how conditional and fragile some relationships truly are.

As I tried to navigate this isolation, another bombshell dropped. We were given a court date for September, but my barrister informed us that she wouldn't be able to attend due to another case that had been scheduled before mine. This left us scrambling to find a replacement, adding even more stress to an already overwhelming situation.

Amid all this chaos, the one constant was my psychologist. He was an incredible support, helping me to confront and process the tangled web of emotions I was experiencing. During our sessions, he encouraged me to acknowledge my feelings—shame, guilt, anger, and sadness—and to begin untangling the threads that had led me to this point. It wasn't easy, but his guidance provided a glimmer of hope in an otherwise dark and uncertain time.

Eventually, we found another reasonably priced barrister—a critical factor since I was flat-broke. A new court date was set for September, but there was still uncertainty about which judge would preside over the case. We prayed it would be someone who would look beyond the crime I committed and see me as a person, someone who could understand the circumstances that had led me to this point.

me as a person, someone who could understand the circumstances that had led me to this point.

As the date approached, my psychologist prepared a detailed report for the court, while the barrister focused on building my case. It wasn't until late the day before the hearing that we finally learned who the judge would be. When my barrister called with the news, her tone was reassuring. She told me that someone must be looking out for me because the judge assigned to my case was known for being fair and thorough. She had a reputation for looking beyond the surface of crimes to understand the reasons behind them. Hearing this brought me a sense of relief—if my barrister was happy, that gave me hope. I had no concept of what made a 'good' or 'bad' judge; this was my first time facing anything like this, and I felt completely out of my depth.

The day of the hearing finally arrived. I left all my belongings at home, fully prepared for the possibility that I might not be coming back. The weight of that decision made every step to the courthouse feel heavier.

In the courtroom, the judge listened carefully to both sides. She reviewed the psychologist's report and asked thoughtful questions, taking everything into account. But to my surprise, she wasn't ready to make a decision that day. Instead, she requested more information. She asked the psychologist to answer an additional seven questions to provide greater clarity before she handed down a sentence. The next hearing was set for November 13, 2019.

Walking out of the courthouse that day, I felt an unexpected mix of emotions. On one hand, I was relieved to have more time, but on the other, the uncertainty stretched on. What would the judge decide? Would the answers in the psychologist's report make a difference? I didn't know, but I knew I had to face whatever was coming with as much strength as I could muster.

So, back I went to the psychologist to address the seven questions the judge had posed. Each session felt heavier than the last as we delved deeper into the issues that had brought me to this point. The goal was to have the answers ready in time for the next court case, but the weight of what lay ahead made it hard to focus.

During one of these sessions, I confessed something I had been grappling with: I still hadn't told my family about the situation. The idea of sitting down

154

with them, especially my mum, and admitting everything was unbearable. Instead, I had concocted a plan to explain my potential absence. I thought of telling them I was going overseas for an extended period, choosing a country where telecommunications were notoriously unreliable so they wouldn't question why I wasn't calling them every day.

When I shared this idea with my husband, he thought it was absurd. He insisted that I couldn't hide this from my family, especially my mum. That I needed to sit down with them and tell her the truth. I knew he was right, but the thought of seeing her disappointment, hurt, and confusion was almost more than I could bear. How could I look into her eyes and admit the shameful reality of what I had done?

The psychologist agreed with my husband, gently reminding me that hiding the truth would only create more distance and pain in the long run. But even with their encouragement, I wasn't sure if I had the strength to do it. For now, I decided to focus on answering the judge's questions and preparing myself for whatever lay ahead.

Two weeks before the court date, I finally mustered the courage to tell my mum. I took her and one of my siblings to lunch, knowing it was now or never. As I began to explain what had happened, the look of pain on her face was indescribable. Her eyes filled with a mixture of disbelief and sorrow. All she kept saying was, 'You never stole, not even a pen from work—how did it get to this?' I had no answer. The weight of her words crushed me, and the silence that followed felt endless.

Despite the pain I caused her, there was a small part of me that was relieved. At least now she knew, and I no longer had to carry the burden of hiding the truth. But even in that relief, guilt gnawed at me. I was grateful my dad wasn't around to witness any of this—I didn't know how he would have reacted, and the thought of his disappointment was too much to bear.

In the days that followed, I tried to spend as much time as possible with Mum. I wanted her to know how much I loved her, even though I had let her down in the worst possible way. She expressed her desire to come to court, wanting to support me, but I refused. I knew I would be a mess, and I didn't want her to see me like that or become more upset. Protecting her from the harsh reality of the courtroom felt like the only thing I could do to lessen her pain.

The night before the court case, on November 12 at precisely 7:31 p.m., I made the difficult decision to text my siblings. I didn't want to leave things unsaid, knowing I was likely going to jail the following day. In the message, I explained what I had done, the decisions that had led me to this point, and my overwhelming regret. Most importantly, I asked them to look after Mum, as she was my greatest concern, aside from my husband and son. I couldn't bear the thought of her struggling through this alone.

The next day, after the court proceedings, the news broke. My story was splashed across page three of one of Melbourne's major newspapers. It spread like wildfire. My husband's phone was inundated with calls and text messages from friends and acquaintances, all wanting to know what had happened. Even his family in Western Australia and Queensland found out through the coverage.

The exposure was mortifying. I had hoped to keep things private, but now it felt like every detail of my life was on display for the world to judge. Watching my family, especially my husband, shoulder the burden of endless questions and prying eyes added another layer of guilt to what I was already carrying. All I could do was brace myself for what came next and hope that, somehow, they would find a way to forgive me.

The following day, my husband and I attended court with one of my siblings, a couple of dear friends who had stood by my side through everything, and my lawyer and barrister. The judge listened to both sides again, carefully considering the psychologist's report. But despite her efforts, she still couldn't decide on the length of the sentence until she had gone through all the documents in greater detail.

The decision was made to remand me in custody until Wednesday, November 27. Everything after that was a blur. Tears streamed down my face as they led me away. I wasn't even allowed to say goodbye to my husband, my sibling, or my friends. The pain of leaving them without a final embrace or word of reassurance was almost unbearable. The only small consolation was that, up until that point, I had not been handcuffed—a small dignity that meant more than I could explain.

Once again, I was placed in the brawler and transported back to Dame Phyllis Frost Centre for another two weeks. The process was just as humiliating as before. I was strip-searched, issued second-hand clothing that was far too big for me, and forced to endure the long wait before being taken to my cell. When I finally arrived, it was the same story—a dirty, unkempt space that reflected a lack of care or pride. Some of the other prisoners didn't seem to care about the conditions, but for me, it was another layer of despair.

To make matters worse, I was placed on death watch, as the authorities were concerned I might harm myself. Every hour, an officer peered into my cell, their presence a constant reminder of how low I had fallen. The lack of privacy was suffocating, but I understood their precautions. The weight of my circumstances was heavy, but I was determined to endure it. I had to— for my family, for myself, and for the hope that, eventually, I could rebuild from the ashes of this experience.

The conditions at Dame Phyllis Frost were as grim as I remembered, and I refused to eat the food served to me. The meals were unappetising, and after hearing countless stories from other inmates about hygiene—or the lack thereof—I simply couldn't bring myself to trust the food. For two weeks, I survived on bottled water, Tim Tams, crackers and cheese, and the occasional piece of fruit.

Every now and then, one of the prisoners who lived in a unit where they could cook for themselves would bring me some food. I didn't accept it every time, knowing how scarce food could be for them, but when I did, it was a small but meaningful gesture of kindness. These small acts of humanity helped make the days a little more bearable.

Until my husband managed to deposit money into my account, another prisoner generously helped me get by. She bought me some water and shared her biscuits and chocolate with me. Her generosity, despite her own limited means, touched me deeply. It reminded me that even in a place filled with despair, there were moments of connection and kindness that could pierce through the darkness.

After two weeks, I was taken back to court to hear my sentence. My husband and family were advised not to attend, as there would be media outside, and they would likely be harassed. It was an unfortunate reality, but I understood the reasoning. However, my client's lawyer hadn't extended the same warning to him, and he was relentlessly hounded by reporters. It was a terrible thing to witness, even from a distance.

Unbeknownst to me, the judge had granted one media organisation permission to record the sentencing, under the condition that the camera would only capture her face, not mine. When an officer informed me of this just before the hearing, I was shocked. She assumed I had already been made aware, but I hadn't. It felt deeply unfair that my name and case were so public, and to make matters worse, despite recording the proceedings, the media still got many details wrong.

As the judge began reading my sentence, I struggled to follow what she was saying. The months and years she mentioned blurred together, and in my confusion, I thought I was going to jail for life. It wasn't until later, when my barrister and lawyer came downstairs to explain, that I finally understood: I had been sentenced to two and a half years on the bottom and four years on top.

Both my barrister and lawyer were pleased with the outcome. They explained that the judge had taken into account my numerous references, my good standing in the community, and the certificates of community work I had received from both state and local governments. My charitable contributions and efforts also played a significant role in her decision. While the sentence still weighed heavily on me, I could see that the judge had made an effort to balance justice with compassion.

Even so, the knowledge that my name and story were now public—misrepresented and sensationalised by the media—was a bitter pill to swallow. The court's decision marked the end of one chapter, but it was clear that another, equally challenging one, was just beginning.

Back in the brawler, I was once again transported to Dame Phyllis Frost Centre. This time, the weight of my sentence pressed down on me, making the ride feel even longer and more suffocating than before. When I arrived, I discovered that my case was all over the TV. Every station carried the story as a breaking news item, complete with different photos of me from past events, smiling alongside various celebrities.

It was surreal, like watching a twisted version of my life being played out for the world to see. The person in those photos seemed so far removed from the one sitting in a prison van, stripped of everything. My public and private worlds had collided in the most devastating way, and I couldn't stop thinking about how my family must be feeling, watching this unfold in real time.

As the gates of the prison closed behind me once more, I knew I had no choice but to endure. The life I had known was gone, replaced with an uncertain and unforgiving reality. But even in the depths of despair, I held on to a faint hope that this wasn't the end—that somehow, someday, I would find a way to rebuild and make things right.

Chapter 17

Behind the Headlines

We arrived at Dame Phyllis Frost Centre, and the routine began again. I was strip-searched and processed through security, a humiliating ritual that now felt disturbingly familiar. Once cleared, I was led into the prison, bracing myself for the weeks ahead.

No sooner had I stepped inside than I was accosted by a group of women. They had seen the newsbreak—my sentence, the amount of money I had stolen, and every detail the media had splashed across their reports. Some of them congratulated me, commenting on how 'lucky' I was to have received such a short sentence. Their words felt like a slap, though I understood they were comparing my sentence to the harsher ones they had received.

But not everyone's reaction was friendly. A few of the women began peppering me with questions. 'How much money do you still have?' one asked. 'Where is it hidden?' asked another. Their tone was unsettling, and I quickly realised this wasn't just idle curiosity—it was probing, calculated, and unnerving.

One of the first things they tell you when you enter prison is to keep your personal information to yourself, especially when it comes to money. Yet here I was, thanks to the media, with every detail of my case laid bare. They knew more about me than I was comfortable with, and it left me feeling exposed and vulnerable.

I didn't know how to respond, so I kept my answers vague and my demeanour neutral. But the unease lingered. It was a stark reminder that prison wasn't just a place of confinement—it was a place where survival often depended on what you said and even more on what you didn't.

Once I realised I would be in that cell for a few weeks, I took it upon myself to scrub it as clean as possible. The walls were grimy, the floor was dusty, and every surface seemed to carry years of neglect. But no sooner had I swept and mopped than the dust returned, seeping through the countless cracks in the walls. These cracks not only let in dirt but also the extremes of the weather—stifling heat during the day and cold drafts at night.

During these two weeks, I had to go through the induction process, which was mandatory for all new inmates. Until this was completed, I wasn't allowed to work. Once I was cleared, I applied to work in the sewing room, where we made tracksuits for men in other prisons. However, we weren't allowed to make tracksuits for ourselves. I also enrolled in a design course, hoping to learn something new, but I was disappointed to find that it only covered basic skills like threading machines and cutting fabric—things I already knew. Frustrated, I decided to quit the course.

The work hours in the sewing room were long and physically draining. Sitting hunched over a machine for hours on end left my back aching, and I found myself relying on Panadol daily to get through the pain. For all this, I earned just $6.95 a day to start with—a stark reminder of the harsh realities of prison life.

After being sentenced, I was finally moved to a self-contained unit with seven other women. I was lucky enough to get a single room, which meant I didn't have to share with anyone. I locked my door every night from the inside, knowing I was sharing the unit with drug traffickers, drug-affected women, and, most unnervingly, murderers. At first, the unit was relatively calm. There was an older woman who kept things under control, and her presence provided a sense of stability.

Unfortunately, after two weeks, she left, and her absence turned the unit into a nightmare. The women began behaving like unruly children, creating chaos at all hours of the day and night. I couldn't cope with the constant noise and disruption, so I asked to be moved. One of the officers, visibly upset when she discovered where I had been placed, told me that the unit was entirely unsuitable for someone like me. After five long weeks in the high-security prison, my request was granted, and I was transferred to Tarrangower Prison, a low-security facility in Maldon, a small Victorian town two and a half hours away from Melbourne.

The move came just two days before Christmas. As if being in a strange place where I knew no one wasn't hard enough, I quickly learned I had missed the day when Christmas food was distributed to the women. As a newcomer, there was little food left for me. All I was given was a few sausages, some bread, a packet of pasta, and a bag of frozen peas. It was a stark and bitter reminder of how drastically my circumstances had changed.

The transfer itself had been gruelling. The brawler's hard, unpadded seat made every bump on the country roads agonising, and by the time we arrived, I felt as though my back might break in two. But the sparse food and loneliness of my first days in Tarrangower stung even more. Christmas, a time I'd always spent surrounded by family and love, now felt like an empty shadow of what it used to be. Still, I tried to remind myself that this was just one more step in a long journey, and somehow, I had to keep moving forward.

Once processed through the system, I was moved to the cell block at Tarrangower. The walk was uphill, and in an attempt to lighten the mood, I joked about needing a concierge to carry our bags. The other women didn't seem amused; my attempt at humour fell flat, and I decided to focus on getting to the top of the hill, struggling under the weight of my belongings.

When I entered the unit, I was appalled by the filth that greeted me. It was far from the fresh start I had hoped for. Dirt and grime seemed to cling to every surface, but I said nothing. Instead, I quietly settled into my cell, determined to make it liveable. I scrubbed every corner until it felt clean enough to breathe.

As I tried to adjust, I made an effort to strike up conversations with the women already living there. One woman, who seemed to consider herself the leader of the group, informed us all—without room for negotiation—that she would be cooking for Christmas. Her tone left no doubt that she expected everyone to fall in line.

Unfortunately, I found her hygiene habits questionable, to say the least. I didn't trust her cooking, and when Christmas Day came, I skipped both lunch and dinner. The food she served didn't look appetising—it was a chaotic mess on a plate, and I couldn't bring myself to eat it. Instead, I nibbled on a couple of plain potatoes, grateful for at least something I could stomach.

The first few days in Tarrangower were challenging. The dirt, the dynamics, and the adjustment to a new environment were far from easy. But I knew I had to find a way to coexist in this strange and unforgiving world, even if it meant navigating situations like these with caution and patience.

The cell I was assigned had its own unique challenges. The curtain on the window kept falling, leaving my room exposed to anyone walking past. When I needed to use the toilet, I went to see an officer to ask if they could fix it. I waited two and a half hours, but nothing happened. Frustrated, I went back to the officer's window to report it again. This time, a different officer was on duty. He was kind enough to come with me and secure the curtain.

Later that same day, as I was walking past the officers' window, the original officer called me over. I approached, expecting nothing more than a casual interaction, but she went off her head, accusing me of 'officer shopping.' I was stunned. I didn't even know what the term meant, so I asked her. She angrily explained that I had gone to another officer to get what I wanted, which she said was not appreciated.

I burst into tears, trying to explain that I had waited over two hours without any response and hadn't intentionally sought out another officer. I simply went back to the same window, and she wasn't there, so I spoke to whoever was. But my explanation fell on deaf ears. This encounter left me shaken and bewildered. It was my first real taste of the pettiness, vindictiveness, and nastiness that seemed rampant among some of the officers in this country prison. They thrived on playing the women against each other, causing unnecessary issues and tension.

Life in the unit wasn't much better. It was filthy, and no one seemed bothered by it. I decided to take it upon myself to clean the common areas, hoping to make it a more livable space. I didn't ask anyone to help—I just got on with it. But my efforts didn't go unnoticed by the self-proclaimed 'leader' of the unit. She complained to an officer, and instead of appreciating the effort, the officer came to me with a reprimand. 'You need to lower your standards,' she said coldly. 'You're in prison.'

I couldn't believe what I was hearing. Instead of encouraging the women to improve their standards, the expectation was that everyone else should sink to the lowest level. It was a mindset I couldn't understand, and it made an already challenging environment feel even more disheartening. But despite their pettiness, I resolved not to let these attitudes drag me down. If nothing else, I would hold on to my own sense of dignity, no matter how out of place it seemed in this world.

The days at Tarrangower were long and uneventful, with very little to occupy the time. The main activity available was gardening, and for those who know me, gardening has never been my forte. Still, to get out of the block and stay occupied, it was a requirement to work and keep busy. I tried my hand at helping another woman in the garden and even spent some time packing coffee into bags for distribution to other prisons. However, the workspace was small, and they could only accommodate a limited number of women each day, leaving me with long stretches of idle time.

I kept asking the operations manager when I could move to a proper unit, as the block I was in was meant to be temporary, with a maximum stay of two weeks. Yet here I was, still waiting, even as other women were being moved within days of their arrival. The 'boss lady' of the block—a woman who had been there for months—confided that she hadn't been moved because they considered her a troublemaker. Her story didn't offer much comfort. I wasn't a troublemaker—I followed the rules, kept my cell clean and tidy, and did what I was told. Yet it seemed like I was being overlooked.

Finally, just over two weeks later, I was moved into a unit. For the first time, I had to share a room with another woman. I had warned them beforehand that I couldn't sleep in complete darkness and needed either the TV on or at least a light. My new roommate seemed agreeable at first, but after just one night of sharing the room with me, she asked to be sent back to the block. It turned out she had never wanted to leave the block in the first place.

Her departure left me with my own room once again, which was a relief. While the situation wasn't ideal, I was grateful for the small comfort of having my own space. It felt like a small win in a place where victories were few and far between.

With the start of the new year, the prison began calling for women to join the Prisoners' Liaison Committee. I decided to put my hand up and was pleased to be accepted. Around the same time, one of the officers running the social committee approached me with another opportunity. She asked if I would take over organising the film nights for the women. Attendance had been abysmal, with only one or two women turning up because they didn't like the previous organiser. Intrigued by the challenge, I agreed.

For my first film night, I managed to get over a dozen women to attend. While I found the turnout disappointing, the officer was ecstatic—it was a record number compared to previous attempts. Encouraged by the small success, I put together a proposal to improve the film nights. My idea was to introduce monthly themes to make the screenings more engaging. The officer supported my proposal, and I got to work.

Meanwhile, I also joined the social committee, which had struggled to be effective in the past. Recognising the need for structure, I drafted a constitution for the committee with the help of the officer and the other committee members, creating a framework that future women could follow. The positions on the committee were set up on a rotating system, allowing everyone an opportunity to take on roles of responsibility. I was honoured to be elected as the first chair of the committee.

However, not everyone welcomed my involvement. Unbeknownst to me, there were several women who already had an issue with me before I had even transferred to this prison. Their resentment stemmed from my perceived 'lenient' sentence. They had stolen far less than I had, yet they had received much harsher sentences. This comparison fuelled their anger and envy, and when I took on leadership roles, it only exacerbated the tension.

For months, they made my life a misery. Their whispers, glares, and passive-aggressive behaviour were relentless. But thankfully, I wasn't entirely alone. I had managed to make a few genuine friends who had my back and stood by me when things got tough. Their support was a lifeline, helping me navigate the hostility while staying focused on the positive contributions I was trying to make.

As the months went on, women began coming to me with various issues they were experiencing, trusting me to bring their concerns to the Prisoners' Liaison Committee. While I took this responsibility seriously, it quickly became apparent that it wouldn't win me any friends among the staff, especially the Operations Manager. Every time I brought up an issue, their response was dismissive: 'That's been brought up before.' It was beyond frustrating—if the problem had been raised repeatedly, then clearly, it hadn't been resolved.

The Operations Manager didn't appreciate being questioned, and my persistence in representing the women made me a target. It felt like I was stuck between two groups—the women who resented my sentence and the officers who didn't like my advocacy. Together, they made my time at Tarrangower some of the worst days I experienced in prison. The bullying was relentless. I tried to keep a brave face during the day, but at night, I cried myself to sleep, overwhelmed by the hostility and isolation.

Things became even harder a few months after my arrival when the prison went into lockdown due to COVID-19. Visits from loved ones were completely suspended, cutting off one of the few sources of comfort we had. The card-making classes I had started attending were also cancelled, leaving me with fewer ways to distract myself from the relentless monotony and emotional strain.

Determined to keep myself occupied, I threw myself into whatever activities were still available. I enrolled in remote study and spent hours reading books, making cards on my own, sewing, and taking on a cleaning job at the medical centre for an hour in the morning and another in the afternoon. Despite these efforts, the days at Tarrangower felt longer and more draining than the ones I had spent at Dame Phyllis.

Each morning, we had to be up by 7:00 a.m. to line up in the lounge with our ID cards. Nights didn't offer much reprieve, as we were locked up at 10:00 p.m.—but not before the officers came through, slamming doors as they went. It was nearly impossible to get to bed early or settle into a restful night because the noise was so disruptive.

Though I tried to adapt and keep my focus on productive activities, the combination of bullying, isolation, and the unrelenting routine left me feeling utterly drained. Each day felt like a battle, but I held onto the hope that this chapter, too, would eventually come to an end.

One bright spot during my time at Tarrangower was my case manager. He was a new officer who had previously worked as a social worker, and his compassionate approach made a world of difference. I felt comfortable talking to him about almost everything—the struggles of prison life, the issues I faced with other women, and the constant tension with the officers. He supported me wholeheartedly, but he wasn't afraid to call me out when I was out of line. I appreciated his honesty and the genuine care he showed, which was rare in an environment like this.

He confided in me that even he found it challenging to work alongside some of the long-term officers. The culture among them was toxic, and many new officers, including himself, struggled to fit in. The long-term staff seemed entrenched in a mindset that prisoners were less than human, and they didn't hesitate to remind us of our place.

I vividly remember an encounter with one officer that perfectly illustrated this attitude. I had asked for some information to help with a thesis I was working on for my studies. Her response was curt and dismissive: 'It doesn't need to be perfect—you're in prison, so it's not important.' Her words stung. I couldn't help but respond, 'What's the point of doing it if it's not to the best of your ability?'

That moment stayed with me. It highlighted the pervasive attitude that because we were prisoners, we didn't deserve to strive for excellence or take pride in our work. But for me, my studies were a way to maintain my sense of self-worth and dignity, and I wasn't about to let their small-mindedness take that away.

My case manager understood this. He encouraged me to keep pushing forward, despite the obstacles, and to focus on what I could control. His support didn't erase the hardships I faced, but it made them a little easier to bear. In a place where kindness was scarce, his presence reminded me that not everyone viewed us as hopeless cases, and for that, I was deeply grateful.

The year passed excruciatingly slowly, but I held onto one glimmer of hope—Christmas. I had been planning for weeks to make the holiday special for the women in my unit. I had volunteered to do all the cooking and had even included a few others in the celebration, including a two-year-old boy who lived in the prison with his mother. Being in a low-security prison afforded us the opportunity to purchase limited items with our own money, so I had been carefully saving and ordering extra food. My aim was to create a meal that, for just a moment, might make us forget where we were.

But someone had other plans for me.

Just a week before Christmas 2020, two women in the compound started spreading a dangerous rumour: They accused me of being a police informer. In prison, this label is not only defamatory—it can be life-threatening. The accusations quickly gained traction, and the situation escalated when a young woman, known for her unusually close relationship with the Operations Manager, approached me. She began putting words in my mouth, claiming I had said I was scared for my life. I vehemently denied it, but it was too late— the damage had been done.

The young woman reported back to the Operations Manager, who immediately ordered that I be placed in solitary confinement while they 'investigated further.' It was a crushing blow. I had been looking forward to celebrating one of the women's birthdays that evening and had prepared a dish to contribute to the party. Instead, I found myself locked away, alone, with no explanation other than the accusations against me.

When the Operations Manager came to see me that night, he assured me the matter would be resolved by the next day. Clinging to his promise, I tried to remain hopeful. But the next day came and went with no word. When I requested to speak with him, I was told he had gone on leave for a few days. It was clear I was being left in limbo, with no recourse and no advocate.

Then the news came—a decision had been made without my input or further investigation.

They were transferring me back to the high-security prison at Dame Phyllis Frost Centre. My heart sank. I had spent months trying to build a semblance of stability in this low-security facility, and now, it felt like it was all being ripped away. The plans I had made for Christmas, the connections I had started to rebuild, and the small progress I had made—it was all crumbling before my eyes.

The sense of betrayal was overwhelming. This was supposed to be a place for rehabilitation, yet it felt like punishment layered upon punishment. The rumours, the manipulation, and the abuse of power by those meant to protect us were stark reminders of the harsh reality of prison life. As I prepared for yet another upheaval, I couldn't help but wonder how much more I could endure.

This turn of events felt like the ultimate betrayal. All my efforts to create a sense of normalcy for Christmas—something that could bring a sliver of joy to those around me—were erased in an instant. The accusations against me were baseless, but in prison, perception is reality, and I had no way to defend myself against the whispers that had turned into decisions made behind closed doors.

As I sat in solitary confinement, the weight of everything pressed down on me. The loss of trust, the isolation, and the harsh reality that I was being sent back to the high-security prison left me feeling defeated. I had clung to the hope that I could rebuild some semblance of a life, but this place had a way of pulling you back down just as you began to rise.

With Christmas just days away, the thought of being stripped of what little comfort I had built was almost too much to bear. I knew I would have to face Dame Phyllis Frost Centre again, and, with it, the harsh routines and rigid walls that had marked my earlier time there. It was a reminder that in this environment, even the smallest glimmers of hope could be taken away in an instant.

Chapter 18

The Price of Standing Tall

COVID-19 restrictions cast an even darker shadow over the already isolating experience of prison life. Face-to-face visits—once a rare but vital source of comfort—were replaced by brief, monitored Zoom calls. Though I was grateful for the technology, these sterile, 30-minute interactions couldn't replicate the warmth and connection of seeing loved ones in person. Every word was scrutinised, every moment felt constrained, making the sense of isolation even more profound.

The restrictions not only widened the emotional chasm between me and the outside world but also deepened the monotony and loneliness of daily life. With fewer opportunities for connection and no meaningful outlets to counteract the bleak routine, the days blurred together in a haze of isolation. The lack of human contact compounded the emotional toll of incarceration, making every small connection with my family a treasured lifeline that I clung to with all my strength.

The following morning, December 16, my world shifted again. The Governor's promise to follow up proved empty. Instead, I was informed that I would be transferred to the Dame Phyllis Frost Centre for 'protection.' The absurdity of the situation left me speechless. One officer even compared my case to Carl Williams, a high-profile inmate—a comparison so ludicrous it felt like a cruel joke. Despite my protests and assurances that the women at Tarrangower didn't believe the rumours, my fate was sealed.

Adding to my heartbreak was missing my friend's 40th birthday celebration. We had spent months planning and gathering small luxuries to create something special in the bleakness of prison life. That night, as I lay alone, the ache of exclusion felt unbearable. Tears slid silently down my face as I pictured the laughter and camaraderie I was missing. Even the food I had contributed felt like a hollow offering, a reminder of my absence from a moment I had longed to share.

As I was loaded into the transfer van, my belongings hastily packed, and my carefully saved Christmas food left behind, I felt utterly defeated. The officer said to me, 'You've been screwed over! They warned us about you when I started,' he admitted. 'Said you were a bully.' I turned to face him, incredulous. 'Do you think I'm a bully?'

He glanced at me briefly before returning his eyes to the road. 'Not at all. From what I've seen, you're polite to everyone. The opposite of a bully.'

His words should have offered relief, but instead, they deepened the sting. I had tried to be a contributor, someone who supported the other women, but it seemed my efforts had painted a target on my back. The officer's candid insight confirmed my suspicion: this transfer wasn't about my safety but about silencing me. 'They don't like women who stand their ground,' he added. 'Especially intelligent ones.'

The comparison he drew between me and the kind of inmate the officers preferred—those who kept quiet and didn't 'rock the boat'—felt like an indictment of everything I had tried to stand for. I sat silently, absorbing his words, the weight of them heavy on my chest.

The gates of Dame Phyllis Frost Centre loomed large as we arrived, cold and unwelcoming. Bracing myself for the humiliating strip search that awaited, a new wave of isolation settled over me. COVID-19 restrictions meant no visits and no real connection to the outside world. The walls felt higher, the barriers thicker. Yet, even in that moment of despair, a quiet resolve took hold. If they thought this would break me, they didn't understand the strength I had spent a lifetime building.

The strip search, as demeaning as it was familiar, marked my introduction to the prison. The indignity of it never lessened. Afterward, I was left to sift through my belongings from Tarrangower, separating what I could keep from what had to be sent home. Despite being on my property list, items like my bed linen, a CD player, a lamp, and other personal belongings were confiscated without explanation. The loss wasn't just emotional—it added to my financial strain, as I would eventually need to repurchase these essentials out of my own pocket. To add insult to injury, my phone credits vanished into thin air, with no reimbursement offered.

The cascade of injustices continued with the discovery that I had been short-paid for my work at Tarrangower. Though the missing wages might seem minor, every dollar mattered in prison. A small sum could mean a phone call to a loved one or the purchase of a desperately needed item. The refusal to address these unpaid wages felt like yet another calculated blow in a system designed to dehumanise.

Determined to reclaim some sense of control, I focused on saving as much of my earnings as possible. I didn't want to burden my family financially and aimed to cover my own needs. Essentials like food, toiletries, and replacements for the confiscated items—like sand shoes and bed linen—took priority. Despite the constraints, I managed to save at least $20 a week, a small but meaningful act of independence in an environment where autonomy was a rare luxury.

Communication, too, came at a price. At Tarrangower, a 15-minute landline call cost nearly $8, and mobile calls were an unaffordable luxury. With a strict $50 monthly phone budget, I limited my calls to brief but cherished conversations with my husband and mum. These moments, though precious, were overshadowed by the constant knowledge that every word was monitored and recorded.

At Dame Phyllis, landline calls were far cheaper—just 30 cents. However, this came with its own frustrations: each call was limited to 12 minutes, forcing me to condense my words into rushed updates, leaving much unsaid. These restrictions underscored the ache of disconnection, making me long for unguarded, uninterrupted conversations with my loved ones.

Not long after settling in, I was transferred to Swan 2 block. Following a medical check that revealed dangerously high blood pressure, I was handcuffed and loaded into a small van. The cuffs bit into my wrists, leaving deep marks that lingered for days. Despite reporting the injury to a senior officer, my concerns were dismissed without action—a stark reminder of how easily our physical well-being was ignored within these walls.

Swan 2 was a grim, crumbling building reserved for prisoners deemed dangerous or defiant. The walls, covered in graffiti, seemed to echo with the despair of countless others who had passed through. The air was damp and cold, the cells filthy. Basic necessities were absent—I wasn't even provided toiletries. When I requested shampoo and conditioner, I was told to wait until the next canteen day, nearly a week away. My bottled water from Tarrangower was also denied. Instead, I was given just four bottles to last an entire week— a meagre supply, especially with my kidney condition.

Even making a phone call was an ordeal. Officers locked me in a tiny, claustrophobic telephone booth at their convenience. My severe claustrophobia made these moments unbearable. Though most officers would release me after my call, one took nearly 30 minutes to respond. By the time the door finally opened, I was curled on the floor, trembling in a fetal position, overwhelmed by panic.

On my first day using the phone, I glanced out at a caged courtyard and noticed a woman pacing. She wore a full burqa, her hands restrained by handcuffs connected by a long steel rod that made even the smallest movement impossible. The sight was chilling. Later, when offered an hour of fresh air, I refused, terrified of being subjected to similar restraints. It took four days—and a supervisor's reassurance that my fears were unfounded—before I cautiously ventured outside.

Despite being placed in Swan 2 for 'protection,' the conditions were anything but safe or supportive. The lack of empathy from the staff, the unsanitary environment, and the isolation weighed heavily on me. Christmas was especially bleak. While my family gathered to celebrate back home, I sat alone in my cell, not even offered a 'Merry Christmas' by the officers. The meal—a plate of thinly sliced turkey, overcooked vegetables, a sweet, and a bread roll—remained untouched. I subsisted on bottled water, crackers, and fruit, unable to stomach the prison food.

The days in Swan 2 blurred into a haze of loneliness and despair. The system wasn't just stripping away my freedom—it was eroding my dignity, piece by piece.

This ordeal was a stark reminder of how effortlessly the prison system could strip away not just freedom, but also dignity. Each day in Swan 2 felt like a battle to maintain my sanity and humanity in an environment seemingly designed to break both. The isolation, the cold sterility of the cells, and the oppressive atmosphere made every moment a test of resilience. It felt as though I was being punished not for my crime, but for refusing to conform to the person they expected me to be.

After more than two weeks in Swan 2, I was transferred to a newer block called Rosewood. The difference was striking—modern, clean cells stood in stark contrast to the decrepit conditions I had endured. Yet, freedom remained elusive. My schedule was tightly controlled: one hour out of my cell in the morning, a brief reprieve at lunch, and another hour late in the afternoon before the final lock-up. I wasn't permitted to go outside, and my movements were confined to the building's general indoor area. The monotony and confinement persisted, albeit in slightly better surroundings.

I later learned I had been placed under an Intermediate Regime, which meant I spent most of the day confined to my cell with only limited access to shared spaces. Even the officers seemed puzzled by my placement, shrugging it off as merely 'following the rules.' On multiple occasions, they forgot to let me out for my allotted hours, compounding my frustration and amplifying my sense of powerlessness.

Desperate for some semblance of purpose, I inquired about the possibility of working. The officers asked what I had in mind, and I expressed an interest in working in the kitchen. After some deliberation, I was granted permission to meet with the kitchen staff—but only under strict time constraints. I had just 20 minutes to reach the kitchen, sign in, and another 20 minutes to return and sign back into my cell. The rush to meet these deadlines highlighted how even the smallest privileges were overshadowed by the regimented structure of the regime.

On January 5th, I began my new role in the kitchen. Initially, I was tasked with washing dishes, a mundane but welcome distraction. The officer overseeing my assignment informed me that I'd need to prove myself for at least a week before being trusted to prepare meals for the other prisoners. While far from glamorous, the work gave me a sense of purpose—an opportunity to reclaim a sliver of agency in a place that so often denied it.

It was during this time that I made a startling discovery. Swan 2 wasn't, as I had been told, a protective unit. It was what the officers called the SLOT—a block reserved for prisoners labelled as difficult, defiant, or disruptive. This revelation confirmed my growing suspicion: my transfer wasn't about protection; it was a deliberate act to silence me. I had challenged the status quo at Tarrangower, advocating for fairness and raising uncomfortable issues. My refusal to 'play along' had made me a target, and my placement in Swan 2 felt like the final piece of a calculated plan to remove me.

After two weeks in Rosewood, I was relocated yet again—this time to Torrens, another locked-down unit. The constant relocations were exhausting, both physically and emotionally, but I tried to focus on the hope that I might eventually find stability. After another two weeks in Torrens, I was finally transferred to a self-contained unit where I was allowed the freedom to cook for myself. This small but meaningful reprieve offered a glimmer of normalcy in an otherwise suffocating environment.

Once I settled into my new unit, I requested several personal items from my property, including my diary, the sand shoes I had purchased at Tarrangower, and my Dior sunglasses. These items were more than mere possessions—they were anchors to my sense of self. My diary, in particular, held deeply personal entries documenting my journey through an unimaginably challenging time.

When the items arrived, my heart sank. Only a few things on my list were included. The diary, shoes, and sunglasses were missing. Attached was a note listing the remaining items, but these three essentials weren't mentioned. I immediately raised the issue, asking where they were. At first, I was told they had already been given to me. When I challenged this, the story changed—they claimed the items had been sent home. Knowing this wasn't true, I asked my husband to check, and he confirmed that they weren't in the bags of items he had taken home.

Frustrated but determined, I continued raising the issue, but each time, my concerns were dismissed or met with indifference. Finally, I decided to escalate the matter. On March 1, I wrote a detailed letter to the prison's General Manager, outlining my efforts to retrieve the missing items. I emphasised the irreplaceable value of my diary and requested either their return or reimbursement.

After waiting for over a month, I received a response. The General Manager claimed she was satisfied with the investigation and insisted that the items had been sent home. Disheartened but unwilling to give up, I wrote to the Ombudsman, meticulously documenting the entire ordeal.

To my surprise, the Ombudsman's involvement brought results. Within a month, an officer and the Property Manager visited me. They handed over my missing items, including my diary, sand shoes, and sunglasses, and even offered an apology. Relief washed over me as I held my belongings again, especially the diary. Still, I couldn't help but feel frustrated by the unnecessary hurdles I had to overcome to retrieve what was rightfully mine. This experience served as a stark reminder of how easily the system could strip away both dignity and control, even in the smallest matters.

During this time, working in the kitchen became a source of solace. After progressing from washing dishes to cooking meals, I found comfort in being productive. The work also introduced me to other women, including one who, like me, was serving time for white-collar crime. We quickly bonded over shared experiences, offering each other support through the challenges of prison life. Our conversations reminded me of the humanity that could still exist within such an unforgiving environment.

In April, my suspicions about the officers at Tarrangower orchestrating my transfer were reinforced. To my dismay, one of the women who had spread the malicious rumours about me was transferred to Dame Phyllis for 'medical reasons' and placed in my compound. I wouldn't have known if not for my new friend from the kitchen, who told me that this woman was already at work spreading the same harmful lies.

The rumours resurfaced, this time claiming I kept a diary documenting the lives of the women around me. Though baseless, the accusation eroded trust, casting a shadow over my interactions with the other prisoners. Determined to address the tension, I called a meeting, laid everything bare, and offered to show them my diary—a deeply personal account of my own thoughts and struggles. Transparency and honesty helped rebuild the fragile trust, restoring a sense of normalcy within the group.

This incident was a powerful reminder of how quickly trust could disintegrate in prison, especially in the hands of those who thrived on manipulation. But it also reinforced something equally important: honesty and direct communication had the power to rebuild that trust, even in the harshest of environments.

After a month of cooking for over 100 women in the prison kitchen, I was approached with an unexpected opportunity. An officer asked if I would like to work in the visitors' café. It was considered a privilege, a position granted to only a select few, and I didn't hesitate to accept. By this time, my daily earnings had reached $8.95—the maximum rate anyone could earn in the system. While it wasn't much, it felt like an acknowledgment of my efforts and reliability.

The kitchen work had been gruelling. The long hours, constant heat, and heavy lifting took a toll on my body. Being a small woman, the physical strain was immense, and I often paid the price with aching muscles and sheer exhaustion. The café job felt like a reprieve, a chance to step away from the relentless demands of the kitchen. When the offer came, I jumped at the chance, grateful for the opportunity to shift to something less physically punishing.

Working in the café also came with a significant level of trust. It meant I would be handling money daily, preparing food for officers, and serving visitors. This responsibility wasn't given lightly, and I took it seriously. The officers seemed to view the women working in the café differently, treating us with a level of respect that was rarely afforded elsewhere in the prison. Perhaps it was the nature of the work or the trust inherent in handling money, but this change in their behaviour didn't go unnoticed.

However, due to COVID-19 and the resulting lockdowns, there were very few days when visitors were allowed. The café, which should have been bustling with activity, often felt eerily quiet, reflecting the pandemic's pervasive impact even within the prison walls. As a result, the only people we served were the officers.

The officers enjoyed access to the best food at unbelievably cheap prices. They were served restaurant-quality meals for just a few measly dollars—meals they often took home to feed their families. The supposed cost of holding prisoners, widely quoted at over $100,000 per year per inmate, felt like a cruel misrepresentation. A significant portion of that money wasn't spent on us—it subsidised officers' lunches, dinners, and take-home meals.

Holidays like Christmas and Easter were particularly disheartening. While we weren't allowed to have visitors on these special days, the officers held parties on the premises. These celebrations were catered by us—the prisoners—using funds from the prison's budget that were meant for our welfare. Cooking for their festivities, knowing I couldn't see my own family, was a stark reminder of the system's inequities and the dehumanising way it operated.

The prison medical system was appalling. Weeks could pass before being seen by a nurse, and seeing a doctor felt like an impossible luxury. This inefficiency became painfully clear when I fell seriously ill with labyrinthitis—an inner ear infection that affects hearing and balance. The symptoms were debilitating: constant dizziness, loss of balance, nausea, vomiting, and a loud ringing in my ear. I could do little more than lie motionless on the couch in the common lounge, unable to move without intense vertigo.

The officers, visibly concerned, repeatedly called for medical assistance. Despite their efforts, no one came. It wasn't until the next day that a nurse finally arrived. Her diagnosis? Vertigo. She assured me I would feel better within a day. But a day passed, then another, and my symptoms showed no signs of improvement. Frustrated and exasperated, the officers called medical again.

The medical system's inefficiencies underscored the systemic neglect prisoners faced daily. After days of advocacy by concerned officers, I finally received the care I needed, a stark reminder of how broken the system was. Yet, amidst the failures, the officers' persistence offered a glimmer of humanity in an otherwise dehumanising environment.

Their persistence eventually paid off, and a doctor was sent to examine me. He quickly diagnosed labyrinthitis, confirming what I already suspected: this wasn't something that would resolve itself overnight. He prescribed medication and instructed that it be brought to me directly, as I was too unwell to make the trip to medical. This exception was rare and highlighted a broader issue—medication was typically only available at the medical centre, requiring prisoners to walk there regardless of their condition. Too bad if you physically couldn't get up; the system didn't care.

While the doctor's intervention brought relief, the experience left me with mixed feelings. The officers' advocacy during this ordeal was remarkable. They went above and beyond to ensure I was cared for, pushing against a system that seemed indifferent to our well-being. For that, I will always be grateful. But it was also a stark reminder of the systemic failures we faced daily—a medical system so broken that even basic care required relentless advocacy and sheer luck.

There were a number of officers at Dame Phyllis who genuinely cared about the prisoners, showing compassion and humanity in a system that often seemed designed to strip both away. Their actions made a difference—whether it was advocating for better medical care, treating us with dignity, or simply listening when we needed someone to hear us. These officers stood out, and I'll always be grateful for their efforts.

One incident in the kitchen starkly highlighted the varying attitudes of the staff. An officer in charge approached me with a bag of yellow, smelly broccoli and instructed me to cook it for the prisoners. The stench alone was enough to turn my stomach. When I inspected the broccoli, I saw it was clearly rotten. I told her I wouldn't feed it to my worst enemy, let alone the prisoners. Her response? 'We can make soup out of it.' I refused, standing my ground, so she left the bag on the bench, insisting she would handle it herself.

As I continued cooking, two other officers passed by my station. Wrinkling their noses, they asked, "What is that smell?" After I explained, they took one look at the broccoli, grimaced, and promptly threw it in the bin. I was relieved—not just because the stench was unbearable, but because someone had done the right thing.

Half an hour later, the original officer returned, looking for the broccoli. When I told her what had happened, she exploded into a rant, insisting she was a trained chef and knew better than the others. To my disbelief, she marched to the rubbish bins, determined to retrieve the rotten vegetables. Fortunately for the prisoners, she didn't find them—they were buried under too much trash.

This incident was more than just a disagreement over spoiled food. It underscored the disparity in how officers treated us. While some genuinely cared, others saw us as less than human, unworthy of even basic decency. In this case, I was grateful for the intervention of the officers who acted with respect and common sense, but the behaviour of the first officer served as a stark reminder of how little some valued our well-being.

As I navigated the contradictions of prison life—the moments of rare humanity juxtaposed against systemic indifference—I came to understand that survival required more than resilience. It demanded an unshakable belief in my worth. Small victories—a recovered diary, trust earned, or a simple act of kindness—became lifelines, reminding me that no system, no rumour, could erase who I was.

This chapter of my life tested every ounce of strength I had. But it also revealed an unexpected truth: in the bleakest of environments, even a single act of kindness, honesty, or courage could spark hope. That hope would carry me forward, guiding me into what lay ahead—a new chapter in my journey toward reclaiming my life and voice.

Chapter 19

A Future Beyond the Walls

Back at Dame Phyllis, I threw myself into anything that would prepare me for life beyond the prison walls. Keeping busy became my lifeline. I enrolled in educational programs, pursued counselling through Gamblers Help, and worked toward a Certificate III in Hospitality. I even wrote a children's book and learned how to turn dialogue into a script. Each task felt like a step toward reclaiming my future, a way to prove—to myself and others—that I was more than the mistakes that had brought me here.

I wanted to be ready for the world outside, ready to repair the damage I had caused and contribute financially to my family after the mess I'd left them in. My ambitions were high: I dreamed of finding a good job, creating stability for my loved ones, and, perhaps, even changing the lives of other women who had been through the prison system. I imagined sharing my story, not as a tale of defeat, but as proof that redemption was possible, even in the most unforgiving circumstances.

But prison had taught me not to get ahead of myself. When the time finally came to apply for parole, I was cautiously optimistic. The thought of leaving this place behind, of stepping into the light after so much darkness, filled me with overwhelming anticipation. Still, I knew better than to assume it was a done deal. Parole wasn't guaranteed—it depended entirely on the parole board's judgment, their perception of whether I was ready to re-enter the world.

The waiting began—a purgatory of uncertainty. Time, already slow in prison, seemed to grind to a halt. COVID lockdowns made it even worse. With even fewer opportunities to engage in activities, I found solace in books. Days spent locked up in my cell stretched endlessly, but I filled the hours devouring book after book. Sometimes, I'd read nearly a book a day, escaping into other worlds when my own felt unbearably small.

I found myself obsessively crossing out dates on my wall calendar, each one marking another day in this confined existence. I knew I still had at least one more Easter, another Christmas, and, hopefully, my last birthday behind bars.

Those milestones loomed large, bittersweet reminders of what I was missing on the outside.

To keep my hope alive, I focused on the positives. My caseworker reassured me that I had done everything right. I had been a model prisoner, staying out of trouble, engaging with every program available, and using my time productively. 'Your chances are good,' they said with confidence. But even with their encouragement, doubt crept in. The stakes felt impossibly high. Would the board see the woman I was striving to become, or would they only see the person I had been?

As the days stretched on, I reflected on how far I had come. Prison had forced me to confront parts of myself I had long avoided—my fears, my flaws, and the ripple effects of my actions. It had stripped away everything familiar, leaving me with nothing but the raw determination to rebuild. That determination now drove me forward, even as I faced the agonising uncertainty of parole. I could only hope the board would give me the chance to prove myself outside these walls.

There is so much more I could say about my time in jail—the experiences, the challenges, and the lessons learned—but dwelling on it would take me down a path I no longer want to walk. I've paid the price for my crime, a price that will remain with me forever. The remorse I feel for hurting one of my dearest clients and the pain I caused my family is something I will carry for the rest of my life.

But as the day of my release drew closer, I felt a growing sense of anticipation—a chance to rebuild, to make amends, and to embrace the life I had been working so hard to prepare for. The thought of freedom, of stepping outside the prison gates and reconnecting with the world, filled me with a mix of nervousness and hope. It wasn't just about leaving jail; it was about reclaiming my life, one step at a time.

With each passing day, the excitement grew. I was ready to face the world, not as the person I had been, but as the person I had become. My past would always be a part of me, but it no longer defined me. What lay ahead was an opportunity—a second chance to live with purpose, gratitude, and an unwavering determination to do better.

In the lead-up to my release, I made the decision to request an early release on the day itself. The thought of facing a media circus outside the jail was unbearable. Reporters had already printed countless untruths during the original coverage of my case, including hurtful innuendos suggesting I hadn't donated the money to charities. I wasn't willing to give them another opportunity to twist the narrative.

To maintain my privacy, I kept the date of my release a closely guarded secret. Only the night before, just prior to being locked up for the evening, did I share the news with a few trusted individuals. This ensured no one could alert the media and turn my release into a spectacle. Walking out of those gates was a deeply personal moment, and I wanted it to remain just that—mine.

My husband arrived at 7:00 a.m. on March 31, 2022, to whisk me away and take me home. My stomach churned with a mixture of excitement and dread. I didn't know what to expect. Driving home felt surreal, almost as if I were in a dream—but not entirely a good one. The world outside the car window looked familiar yet strange, as though I were seeing it for the first time. I sat stiffly, unsure whether to talk or stay quiet, the weight of the past two and a half years pressing down on me

During my trip home I made a call to my mum to see how she was, but I made the decision not to see any of my family for at least a few days after my release. I needed time to gather myself, to process everything before facing them. The truth was, I wasn't comfortable with myself. I felt ashamed and embarrassed, carrying the weight of what I had done and how it had affected them. The thought of seeing their faces, knowing the pain I had caused, filled me with a mix of anxiety and guilt. I wanted to be in a better headspace, to regain a sense of composure before reuniting with them. They deserved that—and so did I.

When we finally arrived home, the sight of my son waiting for me brought tears to my eyes. Hugging him after almost two years of lockdowns due to COVID-19 and separation felt overwhelming—a bittersweet mix of joy, relief, and guilt for the time I had lost with him. He had grown so much, yet to me, he was still my little boy. That embrace was more than a reunion; it was a promise to rebuild, to heal, and to cherish every moment moving forward.

Later that morning, after the bank opened, I went to the Westpac branch on the corner of Swanston and Collins Street in the city. I needed to open a new account to deposit the cheque I'd received from the prison—my savings from the past two and a half years. Handling the cheque felt surreal, a reminder of how carefully I had budgeted every dollar in prison, where money held a different kind of value.

From there, I headed to meet my parole officer in the city. It was my first meeting, the beginning of fulfilling my parole obligations. Walking into that office felt like a step into a new chapter, one where every action mattered and rebuilding my life had to take precedence. By the end of the day, I was both emotionally drained and cautiously optimistic, ready to face the challenges ahead.

Mum organised a family barbecue for that weekend, bringing everyone together in one place. It was the moment I had been both anticipating and dreading—facing everyone at once. Walking into that gathering felt strange, almost surreal. The day itself was pleasant enough; there was laughter, conversation, and the familiar comfort of being surrounded by family. Yet, beneath the surface, the atmosphere felt charged, as though there were unspoken questions hanging in the air. I could sense their curiosity, their desire to understand, but no one voiced it. Instead, we danced around the subject, each of us silently navigating the fragile space between reunion and resolution.

Later that week, I had to wait three days for the cheque to clear, which it did by Friday. Despite the funds being available, I didn't use any over the weekend. On Monday, when I checked my account again, I was shocked to find the balance was zero. The money was gone. Confused, I called the bank to find out what had happened, but they refused to explain over the phone. Frustrated and anxious, I made another trip to the Westpac branch in the city to demand answers.

When I arrived, they informed me that my account had been closed and that a cheque for the remaining balance would be sent out to me. I was stunned. When I asked why the account had been closed, they refused to provide an explanation. It felt like yet another roadblock, another moment where my past seemed to overshadow everything I was trying to rebuild.

This wasn't the first time I had faced rejection from banks. Before even opening the account at Westpac, I had already received letters from Commonwealth, ANZ, and NAB stating that I was not welcome to bank with them. While I understood the reasoning with Commonwealth and ANZ—I had owed them money during my bankruptcy—I couldn't understand why NAB or Westpac had taken the same stance. I didn't owe them anything, so it was a real puzzle to me and added to the frustration of my situation.

Weeks later, I finally received the cheque from Westpac. By then, I was hesitant to trust any bank, but a friend recommended Great Southern Bank, explaining that everything could be done online. Taking her advice, I opened an account with them and deposited the cheque, hoping this time, things would proceed without any more unexpected hurdles.

Frustrated by Westpac's decision to close my account without explanation, I approached the Financial Ombudsman Services to try to uncover the reason. Even they weren't given any information. I was advised that banks are not obligated to explain their actions, leaving me with no answers. However, Westpac offered me $150 as compensation for the inconvenience, provided I shared an account where they could deposit the money. Reluctantly, I gave them my new bank details, accepting the small token as the only resolution available.

But less than a month later, I was blindsided again. Great Southern Bank, where I had just opened my new account, wrote to inform me that I had 30 days to finalise my account as they were closing it as well. I was in disbelief. The cycle was repeating itself, and I felt utterly powerless.

I reached out to everyone I could think of—my parole officer, my counsellor, the Ombudsman again, and several organisations that support people transitioning out of prison. None of them had ever heard of this happening before, and they couldn't offer any solutions. Eventually, I was referred to the National Debt Hotline, where I spoke with someone who seemed genuinely interested in helping. He told me he had contacts at Westpac and would try to find out why this was happening.

Weeks later, he came back with disappointing news: even with his connections, he couldn't uncover the reason for the closures. I was left with nothing but more questions. It felt like I was being judged and punished all over again, not for anything I had done recently, but for the shadows of my past that refused to let me move forward.

Determined to keep moving forward, I opened another account with a different bank and transferred the small amount of money I had into it. For a while, things seemed to settle, and I hoped I could finally leave the chaos behind.

But a few months later, I received a letter from Great Southern Bank. They informed me they owed me a small amount of money—just a few dollars—and requested my bank account details to deposit the refund. I didn't even consider it. Instead, I shredded the letter. After everything I had been through, I wasn't willing to risk giving them my new account information, fearing it would trigger yet another closure and push me back into the same nightmare.

To this day, I can't shake the feeling that something larger was at play. It felt deliberate, as though someone or something was determined to make my life as difficult as possible. I couldn't help but think of the people in Sydney— the same people who had already contributed to my downfall. Were they still pulling strings, ensuring I would never find peace? The thought lingered, a shadow over every step forward I tried to take.

With everything that was happening, I retreated further into myself. I left the house only to visit Mum, attend sessions with my Gamblers Help counsellor, and meet with my parole officer—at first twice a week, then once a week, and eventually just once a month. Each trip out felt like a small battle, and I found solace in the confinement of my own home. It became my refuge—a space that, while isolating, was at least under my control. Even though I was no longer behind bars, I couldn't shake the habit of locking the world out, unsure of how to navigate life on the outside.

It took weeks after my release before I even spoke to friends on the phone. The thought of reconnecting felt overwhelming, like stepping into a world that had moved on without me. Slowly, I began to adjust, taking one small step at a time.

A few months later, I found the courage to start looking for work. I sent out countless applications and resumes to prospective employers, each one accompanied by a cover letter that held nothing back. I told the truth about my past, unwilling to waste anyone's time if they didn't hire people with a criminal record. Each submission felt like an act of vulnerability, a gamble on whether someone could see beyond my mistakes and give me a chance to rebuild my life.

The jobs I applied for were perfect for me—I could have done them with my eyes closed. But rejection after rejection came, each one a painful reminder of the barriers my past had created. Eventually, I gave up chasing my dream roles and decided to apply for something simpler. I applied to the Australian Electoral Commission to work during the state election, handing out pamphlets. It wasn't glamorous or challenging, but I just wanted someone to give me a chance.

I went through the application process, ticking the box that asked if I had a criminal record, and to my surprise, I got the job. For the first time, someone was willing to take a chance on me. I was thrilled and felt a small spark of hope reignite. Within days of being accepted, I received my training manual and began preparing for the role. It was a minor job, but it felt like a step forward.

Then, just a few days later, I received a phone call from the supervisor. She asked me about my criminal record, and I replied truthfully, thinking I had already been transparent during the application process. Her response blindsided me: They had to retract the job offer. I couldn't believe my ears. I was crushed.

Through my frustration, I asked her, 'What do they think I'm going to do? Steal the pamphlets?' She was apologetic, clearly uncomfortable, and explained that it was out of her hands—she had to follow protocol. I hung up the phone feeling defeated, my hope snuffed out once again by a system that seemed determined to hold me back no matter how hard I tried to move forward.

You can imagine what happened next—I shut myself away. I retreated into myself and put myself in jail once again, only this time it was within the confines of my own home. The rejection was a brutal reminder that my past still controlled my future, no matter how much I tried to move on.

So, after spending two and a half years in a physical jail, I added another two and a half years of self-imposed confinement, turning my home into my new prison. The walls of my house became the bars I couldn't escape, built from shame, fear, and a deep sense of hopelessness. It wasn't the system holding me back anymore—it was me.

Locking myself away at home, I realised I needed a hobby—something to occupy my time and give me a sense of purpose. During my time in jail, I had discovered a love for making cards, so I decided to continue that within the confines of my home. I spent countless hours watching YouTube tutorials, honing my craft, and creating personal cards for myself and my family. I only charged for the cost of materials, but the effort and care I poured into each card were immeasurable. It became my little escape, a way to express myself and bring joy to others in a small but meaningful way.

At the same time, I started engaging with social media under a different name, finding a safe space to connect with others and contribute to various pages. There was one particular Facebook group where I became especially active, sharing images and information regularly. My contributions didn't go unnoticed—before long, I was asked to become an administrator for the group. I accepted, throwing myself into the role and helping grow the group's membership tenfold. For the first time in a long while, I felt like I was part of something bigger, contributing in a way that gave me a sense of achievement and connection.

But this newfound connection was short-lived. One of the administrators, for reasons I still don't fully understand, began digging into my background. It seemed she wasn't happy that my posts consistently gained more engagement than hers in the group. What she discovered sent everything spiralling. She found out who I was and what I had done, and instead of confronting me privately, she shared the information with the other two administrators. That's when the bullying began.

It was relentless. They mocked me, ostracised me, and even compared me to Melissa Caddick—the woman whose disappearance made headlines, only for her partially decomposed foot to wash up on a beach months later. The comparison was cruel and completely unwarranted, but it didn't stop them. The constant ridicule and hostility sent me into a spin, reopening wounds I had worked so hard to heal. I had thought I was finally moving forward, but this experience felt like I was being dragged backward, drowning in the weight of judgment and shame all over again.

The bullying broke me in ways I hadn't expected. It wasn't just the cruelty—it was the feeling of being hunted, judged, and reduced to my past mistakes yet again. I had hoped that in the anonymity of social media, I could find a fresh start, a place where I could contribute without the weight of my history hanging over me. Instead, it became another prison of shame, one I couldn't escape.

Eventually, I went silent. I didn't shut down my accounts; I just stopped engaging. The thought of logging in filled me with dread. I felt silenced, as though the very space I had once found solace in had turned against me. The experience was a painful reminder that not everyone is willing to let you move on, but it also taught me something valuable: I couldn't keep looking for validation in others. If I was going to rebuild my life, it had to start from within.

Retreating once more into my own space, I realised it was time for a new approach. The setbacks and the cruelty I had faced only solidified one thing—I needed to take control of my own narrative, not let others define it for me.

Chapter 20

A Year of Loss and Love

Getting through that dark year wasn't easy. It required confronting the pain head-on and finding the strength to keep going, even when it felt like the world was determined to hold me back. Slowly, I began to rebuild—not by erasing the past, but by choosing not to let it define me.

I started small, finding comfort in simple joys: creating cards, engaging in quiet routines, and rediscovering my purpose. I focused on the things I could control and sought out opportunities to contribute in meaningful ways. It wasn't an instant transformation, but with each passing day, I began to feel a little stronger, a little more like myself again.

The journey to this realisation, however, had been anything but easy. In January 2023, the same reporter who had written the initial article about my arrest in 2019 decided to dredge up the story again, this time calling me a 'degenerate.' I wouldn't have even known about it if not for a message on Facebook from someone who recognised me by my real name. They asked, 'What's this all about?' That message hit me like a punch to the gut. Between this public attack and the relentless bullying I had endured from the three administrators on Facebook, I felt completely defeated. Once again, I locked myself away, withdrawing into the safety of my home, unable to face a world that seemed determined to define me by my worst moments.

But as the year drew to a close, something within me shifted. I realised that hiding wasn't the solution—it only gave more power to those who tried to tear me down. Determined to start anew, I enrolled in a Diploma of Event Management at university. With over 40 years of experience in the industry, I saw an opportunity to share my knowledge and teach others the skills I had honed over decades. It felt like reclaiming my identity, transforming the pain of the past into something meaningful and productive.

By Christmas 2023, I made a firm decision: I would no longer lock myself away. I had spent far too long letting fear, shame, and the opinions of others dictate my life. If people couldn't accept my past, that was their issue—not mine. I was done living in the shadows of my mistakes. It was time to step into the light, take control of my story, and embrace a fresh start. 2024 would be my year!

As I stepped into 2024 with determination and hope for a fresh start, life dealt me an unimaginable blow.

The year began on a sombre note, marking a turning point I'll never forget. In late October 2023, my dear mum was diagnosed with pancreatic cancer—a cruel illness that gave us little time to prepare for the inevitable. By January 22nd, she passed away at the Olivia Newton-John Wellness Centre, just a week after my birthday.

Although we knew it was coming and were grateful that she didn't endure prolonged suffering, her loss devastated me. She wasn't just my mum—she was my unwavering rock, my one consistent support, the person who always had my back, thinking of me and my family in ways no one else could. Now, she was gone.

Almost a year later, her absence is a void I feel every single day. I still catch myself reaching for the phone, ready to call her, as I did every single day—sometimes more than once. It was our ritual, a constant in my life, and letting go of that habit has been one of the hardest things.

We had been hoping—praying even—that she would make it to April when we planned to celebrate her 90th birthday. But fate had other plans. She left us just four days before what would have been her 66th wedding anniversary with my dad, reuniting with him after so many years.

The last weeks of her life were heart-wrenching. Cancer had ravaged her body, leaving her frail and unrecognisable, just skin and bones. Yet even in those final moments, she radiated a quiet strength that I will carry with me forever.

This chapter is a tribute to her—a woman whose love shaped me, whose absence has reshaped me, and whose memory continues to guide me as I navigate this new chapter of my life without her.

My ambitions didn't stop there. Along with rebuilding my life, I felt a deep need to address the harm caused by gambling addiction—not just to individuals, but to their families, friends, and the wider community. I wanted to spread awareness and start conversations that could spark real change. I didn't know where to begin or how to approach such a daunting mission, but I was determined to figure it out.

It wasn't just about picking up the pieces of my own life; it was about making a difference. For the first time in years, I felt a sense of purpose stirring within me—a drive to use my experiences to help others and transform my pain into power. The path ahead wasn't clear, but I was ready to take the first steps. I had spent long enough hiding; now, it was time to live.

Talking to my Gamblers Help counsellor became a pivotal moment in this journey. She connected me to the RESPIN Program Coordinator, and during an incredible conversation, I shared my story. She believed I would be a valuable addition to their pool of speakers. RESPIN focuses on raising awareness about the harm caused by gambling, reaching out to organisations and individuals alike. The idea of using my experiences to help others resonated deeply with me, and I knew this was an opportunity I couldn't pass up.

Around the same time, another serendipitous opportunity came my way. I applied to a sponsorship program in the United States designed to help individuals share their stories and participate in a docuseries. The program sought to amplify voices like mine—stories of resilience, transformation, and the power of change. To my astonishment and delight, I was accepted.

This sponsorship not only gave me the platform to share my journey but also provided the support I needed to bring this book to life. Thanks to their generosity, this book exists, and I am forever grateful for their belief in me and my story. It stands as a testament to the power of second chances and the incredible people who dedicate their lives to helping others rebuild theirs.

During this time, I had to rely on my husband for financial support, as finding work proved impossible. To add to the strain, I was refused financial assistance by the government because my husband earned over $80,000 per year. What they didn't consider was our large mortgage or the fact that we had a son still attending university who required financial support. It felt like yet another barrier, one that added to the weight of our circumstances. Despite this, my husband stood by me, and his support allowed me to keep moving forward.

Back at RESPIN, I completed the application process, underwent training, and was eventually accepted as one of their speakers. It was a significant milestone—not just because I was helping others, but because I was reclaiming my voice and turning my pain into something meaningful. For the first time in a long while, I felt like I was truly moving forward.

At the same time, I began studying for my Diploma of Event Management. Balancing my coursework with my growing speaking commitments was challenging, but the sense of purpose both pursuits gave me far outweighed the exhaustion. In May 2024, I came across a free program called the Craft Your Keynote Speech Challenge—a five-day course aimed at helping emerging speakers refine their keynote skills. Intrigued, I eagerly signed up, eager to enhance my abilities.

The experience was transformative. I found myself captivated by the program and couldn't stop talking about it. Feeling inspired and motivated, I approached my husband about enrolling in the paid version. It was a significant investment, but I knew it was a necessary step to take my message beyond the RESPIN program and reach a broader audience. With his support, I enrolled, determined to grow—not just as a speaker, but as a voice for change, sharing the harsh realities of gambling addiction and its ripple effects on families, communities, and individuals.

Through RESPIN, I've had incredible opportunities to speak at various events, connecting with diverse audiences to raise awareness about the harm caused by gambling. These engagements included speaking to counsellors, community groups, and organisations such as Headspace, the Salvation Army, and Banyule Community Health. Each event allowed me to share my journey while offering insights into recovery, resilience, and the crucial role of support systems.

I've also been fortunate to expand my public speaking to broader platforms beyond RESPIN. I've had the privilege of presenting at Melbourne University, Swinburne University, and the Mind Body Spirit Festival, among other community and academic events. These experiences enabled me to connect with people from all walks of life—students, professionals, and everyday individuals—many of whom found hope or strength in my story.

Each speaking engagement feels like a meaningful step toward creating real change. Whether I'm addressing a small group of counsellors or standing before a large festival audience, I've come to realise the profound impact my story can have. It has the power to inspire, educate, and spark critical conversations. These opportunities haven't just provided me with a platform—they've reignited a sense of purpose, fuelling my drive to continue sharing, learning, and growing as a speaker and advocate.

The skills and confidence I've gained through my university diploma also enabled me to return to event management with renewed passion. I organised several events, including a conference for university students and a charity function to raise funds for the Make-A-Wish Foundation. Both projects combined my professional expertise with my personal mission to make a positive impact. One of the highlights of my year was working on the Victorian State Schools Spectacular at the John Cain Arena, collaborating with a team of extraordinary musicians and artists. The experience reminded me of the magic of creativity and the strength of teamwork.

I also had the honour of organising a conference for Kaley Chu at the Melbourne Exhibition and Conference Centre. This event allowed me to showcase my event management expertise while reconnecting with the dynamic world of high-calibre events. Being back in my element felt incredibly rewarding and reaffirmed that my skills remain sharp and relevant.

Another transformative chapter of my journey has been joining the Get Paid to Speak and Inner Circle Program communities. These programs have not only elevated my confidence as a speaker but also introduced me to a network of supportive and inspiring individuals from around the globe. For the first time in a long while, I felt genuinely accepted—judged not for a mistake in my past, but valued for who I am today. Their encouragement has been a beacon of hope, pushing me to keep striving for personal and professional growth.

Adding to these accomplishments, I had the privilege of contributing a chapter to *My Unforgettable*, a collaborative book that became a bestseller in the U.S. and Canada. While the accolades belong to the 12 other incredible women who shared their stories, being part of such a meaningful project is a milestone I treasure. Calling myself a bestselling author is a title I wear with pride—it symbolises not just achievement but the power of shared resilience and collective storytelling.

Looking ahead, 2025 is the year I plan to bring everything I've learned—my successes, setbacks, and decades of experience—into something truly transformative. I will launch my online event management course, a platform designed to teach future professionals the art and science of creating unforgettable events. My dream is not only to inspire the next generation of event managers but also to create a sustainable way to share my expertise while empowering others to build meaningful careers.

But my vision extends beyond the world of events. I dream of a future where women leaving prison are met with opportunities rather than obstacles—a world where their potential is nurtured, their mistakes aren't held over them forever, and second chances are backed by real support. Too often, these women are stigmatised, rejected by employers, and even abandoned by their families. Without access to meaningful education or job training during incarceration, many leave prison unequipped to re-enter society, falling into cycles of homelessness and re-offending.

I've experienced this harsh reality firsthand. Despite a long and successful career, I faced rejection after rejection because of my criminal record. For many women, the struggle is even more daunting. They leave prison without a safety net, practical skills, or a clear path forward. It's a system designed to fail them, trapping them in a cycle of hopelessness and despair.

During my sentence, I met countless women who weren't criminals at heart but had made one mistake—just like me. They were mothers, daughters, and professionals who deserved a second chance. Yet, the system offered them little more than stigma and hopelessness. I often wondered why there wasn't more focus on equipping these women with real-world education, career skills, or entrepreneurial tools—resources that could genuinely help them rebuild their lives and reclaim their futures.

That realisation planted a seed. If I could break free from the shame and rebuild my life, maybe I could inspire others to do the same. And maybe, just maybe, we could demand a better system together—one that empowers women to rise above their past and build brighter futures.

This has become my mission: to advocate for second chances and meaningful reform—not just because it's the right thing to do, but because I've lived the reality of what it means to be judged by your worst mistake. What if incarceration wasn't just about punishment but also about rebuilding? What if, instead of leaving prison with nothing but stigma, women could walk out with a diploma, a job offer, and a support system ready to help them thrive?

The system needs to change. Education and career training should be the cornerstone of incarceration. Women deserve access to diplomas, certifications, and even university courses while serving their sentences. Imagine the dignity and hope this could restore. Beyond education, job placement programs could partner with organisations willing to provide internships and practical skills training. These small shifts could make a world of difference.

And then, there's the transition back to society. Too many women leave prison with no home to go to, no one to guide them, and no safety net to catch them. Housing assistance, mentorship programs, and mental health support aren't luxuries—they're necessities. Without them, the cycle of homelessness and re-offending will never end.

Change also requires a shift in how we think. Employers need to see the value in hiring individuals with lived experience. These women bring resilience, loyalty, and a strength forged through hardship. Policymakers need to rethink incarceration itself—not as a place of shame, but as an opportunity to equip women for success.

This isn't just about compassion; it's about building stronger, safer communities. When we give women the tools to rebuild their lives, we change the trajectory not just for them but for their families, their communities, and society as a whole.

Looking ahead, I dream of standing on the TEDx stage, sharing a vision of empowerment and second chances with the world. I see a future where women leave prison with more than just regret—where they walk out with a diploma in hand, a job offer waiting, and a network cheering them on. This isn't a fantasy; it's a possibility. But it requires all of us to demand better from the system and to stop defining people by their worst moments.

To employers: Please take a chance on women with lived experience. Their resilience and strength can transform your team. To policymakers: Equip women to succeed on the outside, not just survive on the inside. And to everyone reading this: Ask yourself how you can help break the cycle.

As I reflect on the journey that has brought me here, I am deeply struck by how far I've come—from the darkest depths of despair to a life driven by purpose, resilience, and hope. The road hasn't been easy, yet every challenge has taught me invaluable lessons: the importance of self-belief, the power of second chances, and the undeniable truth that no matter how difficult the circumstances, it's never too late to rebuild.

To the critics who doubted me, judged me, or tried to define me by my mistakes: You became my motivation. Your scepticism lit a fire in me to prove that redemption is possible and that people can rise above their past. While your words caused pain, they also strengthened my resolve to succeed and help others do the same.

To the supporters who believed in me when I couldn't believe in myself: You are the reason I am here today. Your kindness, encouragement, and unwavering faith gave me the courage to keep going. I will forever be grateful for the light you brought into my darkest moments. Your belief in second chances has shaped not only my life but also the lives of those I now strive to help.

Looking forward, I see a future brimming with possibility. The dreams that once felt distant—launching my online event management course, stepping onto the TEDx stage, and advocating for systemic change—are now tangible goals within my grasp. I am driven by a deep desire to inspire others, to teach, and to ensure that no one facing adversity ever feels alone.

It's incredible to think how far I've come. Nearly seven years ago, I made the life-changing decision to walk away from gambling—a decision that has brought me to this moment. Staying clean has been one of the hardest but most rewarding journeys of my life. Every day, I am reminded of the strength it took to reclaim my life, and that strength continues to guide me as I step into this new chapter.

But this is not the end; it's the beginning of a new chapter. My story will continue to evolve, shaped by the lives I touch, the lessons I learn, and the change I hope to create. To anyone reading this, I leave you with one heartfelt message: Your past is a part of you, but it does not define you. It may leave its mark, but it doesn't hold the power to limit your future—that power lies entirely in your hands.

As I close this chapter, I do so with immense gratitude—for the journey that brought me here, for the doubters who unknowingly became my motivation, and for the unwavering supporters who lifted me when I was at my lowest. It is my hope that my story serves as a beacon, a reminder that even in life's darkest moments, the light of hope and possibility can guide us forward.

With hope in my heart and purpose in my soul, I step into the next chapter, ready to embrace whatever lies ahead.

About the Author

Connie Paglianiti

Connie is a former event manager with four decades of unparalleled success in orchestrating exclusive events for Hollywood's elite and spearheading significant fundraising efforts for numerous charities. Known for an impeccable track record and the ability to create unforgettable experiences, Connie has been at the forefront of luxury event planning, working closely with A-list celebrities and influential figures to make a lasting impact on various causes.

However, life's unpredictable nature led Connie down a challenging path. A complicated entanglement with a business partner resulted in overwhelming debt, pushing Connie towards crime and gambling as means of escape. This period of turmoil culminated in incarceration, marking a profound turning point in Connie's journey.

Today, Connie stands as a beacon of hope and resilience. Transforming personal adversity into a mission for good, Connie is the creator of a forthcoming podcast dedicated to helping individuals navigate the perils of addiction. By sharing insights, resources, and stories of recovery, Connie aims to provide support and encouragement to those struggling to find their way back.

In addition to the podcast, Connie is penning a deeply personal biography detailing the rise to prominence, the fall from grace, and the path to redemption. This work promises to be a candid exploration of the highs and lows of life, offering lessons on resilience, accountability, and the power of change.

Through these new ventures, Connie seeks not only to address past mistakes but to pave a way forward for others by shedding light on the complexities of addiction and the possibility of a second chance. Join Connie on this journey of reflection, recovery, and renewal.

Linkedin: https://www.linkedin.com/in/conniemarieroberts/

Facebook:https://www.facebook.com/BreakingChainsNavigatingLife/

Instagram: https://www.instagram.com/breakingchains2024/

More Than a Book—A Movement

From the Shadows into the Light is more than just my story—it's a movement for anyone who has ever felt lost, unworthy, or beyond redemption. I want you to know: **you are not alone.**

But this conversation isn't just for individuals—it's also for **corporates, business leaders, and decision-makers** who are ready to **rethink how they support, employ, and empower those who have fallen through the cracks.**

Through my work at **WeSocialise**, corporate workshops, and **speaking engagements**, I work with businesses, organizations, and communities to create **real pathways for change** based on the *4 E's: Empowerment, Employment, Environment, and Education.*

- **Empowerment** – Breaking the stigma and building confidence in those who need a second chance.

- **Employment** – Helping businesses see the potential in hiring individuals with lived experiences, creating meaningful opportunities.

- **Environment** – Shaping inclusive, understanding workplaces that foster resilience and trust.

- **Education** – Providing training, awareness, and resources to change perceptions and drive transformation.

How You Can Get Involved

🩶 **Join the Chainless & Fearless Community** – A space for support, encouragement, and real conversations about healing and growth.

▪️ **Corporate Partnerships & Workshops** – Let's work together to create a **more inclusive workforce** that values **second chances and real transformation.**

🎤 **Book Me for Speaking Engagements** – I share my story and strategies for resilience, breaking stigma, and creating second chances—perfect for conferences, leadership teams, and community events.

Take the Next Step – Visit my website for **free resources, courses, and personal insights** on rebuilding and moving forward.

Let's Connect – Your story matters. Let's start a conversation— whether through social media, a message, or by simply sharing this book with someone who needs it.

You Are Stronger Than You Know

I know what it feels like to think you've lost everything. But I also know what it feels like to rise again. If you take nothing else from this book, take this: **you are not broken. You are not beyond repair. You are worthy of happiness, hope, and a fresh start.**

Website: www.conniepaglianiti.com | www.wesocialise.com.au
Email: Reach out anytime for **collaborations, speaking, or corporate training.**
Stay Inspired: Sign up for my **newsletter** for encouragement, resources, and updates.

This is more than a book. It's a movement. It's a promise that second chances are real.

Together, we break the chains. Together, we rise.

Your past does not define you—your strength does. Your mistakes do not limit you—your willingness to grow does. Whether you are here to **rebuild your own life** or to **be part of a movement that changes lives**, know this: **we are all capable of transformation.**

It's time to step forward—Chainless & Fearless.

With resilience, hope, and unwavering belief in second chances,
Connie Paglianiti

#ChainlessAndFearless